Life...

and That Other Thing

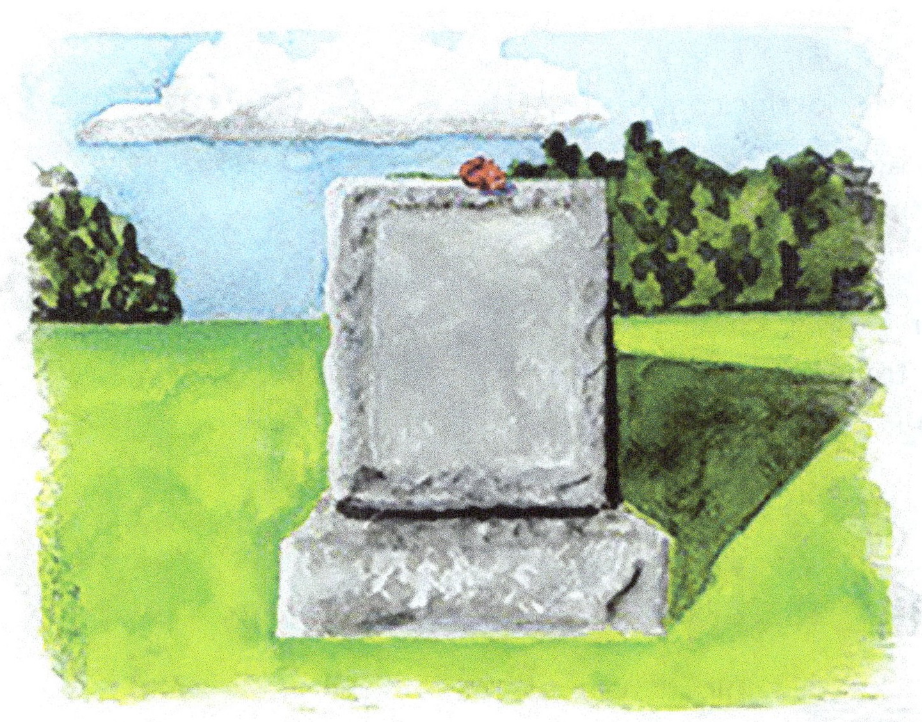

JOHN NIEMAN

Gotham Books

30 N Gould St.
Ste. 20820, Sheridan, WY 82801
https://gothambooksinc.com/

Phone: 1 (307) 464-7800

Published by Gotham Books (November 30, 2023)

ISBN: 979-8-88775-776-6 (P)
ISBN: 979-8-88775-777-3 (E)

Because of the dynamic nature of the Internet, any web addresses or links contained in this book may have changed since publication and may no longer be valid.

The views expressed in this work are solely those of the author and do not necessarily reflect the views of the publisher, and the publisher hereby disclaims any responsibility for them.

For Scott,
who first encouraged me to tackle this topic

Contents

I had promised to meet my sons, my ex-wife, and her new husband after my diagnosis at Memorial Sloan Kettering.

"It looks like pancreatic cancer," the doctor advised about three hours earlier. As I walked to the fun, noisy, and lively P.J. Clarke's in Lincoln Center, I thought about my plight. True, it wasn't a 100 percent certain diagnosis. As I reassured myself, the doc only admitted that it looked like the worst cancer one can fear. However, the prediction rang in my ears. I had to admit to myself that I had never really confronted my own mortality. Yeah, my mom and dad died, but they were old. Not me! And yet, at a point like this, one must at least consider the great beyond.

As luck would have it, after a year and a half of tests, it turned out to be a misdiagnosis (hard for MSK to admit). I now appear to be cancer-free, but that doesn't mean I will live forever. After that scare, I realized I could get hit by a car tomorrow or have a heart attack or get some other exotic disease in Bangladesh.

Backdrop: For years, I had painted and exhibited work all over the world. I had also written more than fifteen books. On the heels of this reprieve, I redoubled my efforts and showed artwork throughout Europe and wrote three more books—almost as if I was unconsciously on borrowed time.

As my son Scott told me after the ordeal, "Well, this is a subject for a book, don't you think?" Maybe. But no one wants to confront the end of their days prematurely. I realize that. So I wrote this not as a maudlin address on dying (although I think that topic is important).

Instead, I have written this a group of fictitious short stories. Flash fiction, if you have heard of the genre. Often, I have combined it with a piece of original art.

Some of the pieces are funny. Some are even silly. I predict some of them may even make you laugh.

Of course, some of them are emotional. In my final analysis, I conclude that nothing is more important. Passing your driving test? Seeing the latest Marvel adventure movie? Going to some crowded bar to see if you can get lucky tonight?

My conclusion: Live every day. Find inspiration around you. If you are aware, and look to the right and then to left, you will find it. One day at a time.

The vast majority of stories and art pieces in this book are fresh and 100 percent original.

However, there are a few that I have borrowed from my previously published books. I steal from no one other than myself. Often, I have changed the story slightly, or revised the artwork. As I retrospectively look back on the canon of my creativity, I did realize that some pieces fit so nicely in this new theme it would be wrong and, perhaps, even selfish to exclude them.

Other than that, I acknowledge that Google, Chrome, and other Safari sites are invaluable in researching the times and the details of relevant events. In the process of researching the topic, I did visit some funeral homes and have a consultation with my local priest, who explained the process he goes through to explain the meaning of one's life when people finally reach that final curtain. Thanks, Father Tim.

I do, however, believe that the entire approach of this tome will feel fresh and brand-new.

Tears in Heaven

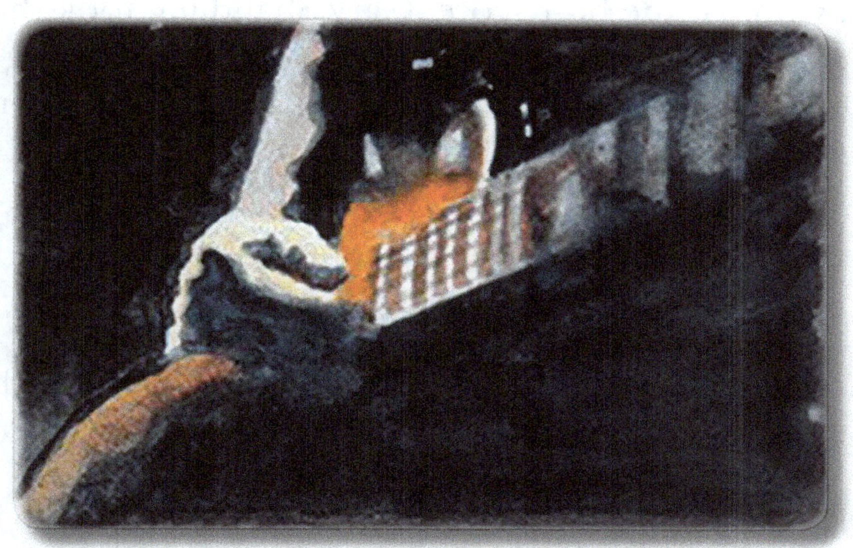

It was the first time I had ever been to the Grammys. As one who had dabbled in music in the aftermath of 9/11, I was invited to attend, and I fully admit to being star struck. There was Beyoncé on the red carpet and Katy Perry. Toni Braxton was next and then Michael and Janet Jackson. Wow! No wonder this event attracts such numbers throughout America.

The year was 1993, and Gary Shandling was the emcee. He was funny and sarcastic as usual. He teased that *Beauty and Beast* was up for the best musical track, and that Emmylou Harris, K.D. Lang, and Sergio Mendes were also nominated. "Oh, also Eric Clapton will be singing a song for you." Suddenly, the party atmosphere took a more serious tone.

Most of us in the audience had heard his emotional hit called "Tears in Heaven" and were secretly rooting for him.

I can't imagine a worse thing than losing your preschool kid who falls out of a window in NYC to his sudden death. And yet it happened at 11:00 a.m. on a sunny morning when the maid had left a window wide open. Evidently, Eric Clapton was nowhere near the apartment, but he was scarred for many months. In fact, he took nine months off from the tour to try to recover from the disaster.

After the rah-rah emotionally stirring theme song from *Beauty and Beast*, which won for the best score, Gary Shandling took the stage and introduced the next entry for best song of year. "It's a song written by Eric Clapton and Will Jennings. The title? 'Tears in Heaven.' Here to play it for you is the one and only Eric Clapton."

In total darkness and thunderous applause, a spotlight eventually illuminated Mr. Clapton, who began strumming and singing.

Would you know my name if I saw you in heaven?

The crowd roared, and Clapton atypically just played chords until the applause petered out.

Would it be the same if I saw you in heaven?

As I listened to the lyrics, I couldn't help but reflect on the awful event. Evidently, the young boy fell on the rooftop of the nearby building. The maid tried to call 911 to retrieve the young lad. Unfortunately, Conor's death was sudden and final.

At the time, I was the father of a three-year-old boy. Instinctively, I closed my eyes and tried to imagine the nightmare as I listened to the uncomfortable, immensely personal lyrics.

At the end of the song, there was a standing ovation for Eric Clapton. Wisely, he humbly accepted the honor without mentioning the event. He simply held up the Grammy and blew an air-kiss to the crowd.

He performed the same ritual for his other four Grammys that night:

Best record.

Best album. Best pop vocal.

Best … best … best … best.

Unlike the usual Elton John "Goodbye Yellow Brick Road" or

Michael Jackson "Thriller" extravaganzas, it was a subdued night, especially in view of the fact that the most honored star sang about his deceased preschool-age son.

However, it made the congregation proud that it was not all about glitter and glamour. Of course, it didn't stop any of us from celebrating later on that night at the Beverly Hills Hotel. At about three in the morning, I returned to my room and paid my babysitter generously. I also hugged my young three- year-old and was forever thankful for every single day I would have with him.

I also closed all the windows, just in case.

Occasionally, I listen to the song by Eric Clapton and thank my lucky stars that no accident has ever befallen any of my five kids. It can always happen. But it never has. And for that, I hope I never have to shed tears in heaven.

2
The Long and Winding Road

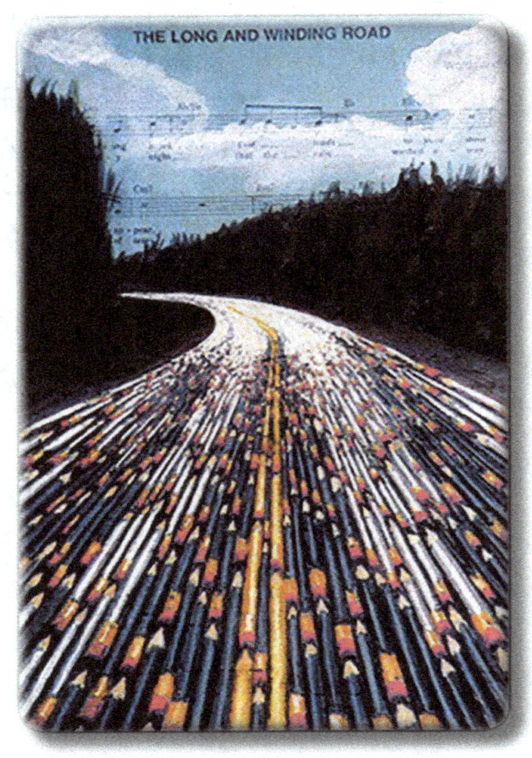

Ever since she had been in high school, Abby Rhodes wanted to be a writer. However, as you may have discovered yourself, sometimes life gets in the way. It has a mind of its own and does not honor your personal agenda. The unexpected occurs, and that calls for a change of plans—or, at the very least, a postponement.

As a high school honors senior in Philadelphia, that's exactly what happened to Abby. She had intended to attend Temple University, but an unexpected pregnancy at age eighteen diverted those plans. She was raised in a conservative family and wouldn't think of an abortion. By the same token, her right-wing father disowned her and suggested that she find a new place to live far away from the "shame" of her misdeeds.

She chose Boulder, Colorado—a rather free "live and let live" area where she could raise her baby in the fresh air and probably easily secure a job at one of their many restaurants. Fortunately, on her first interview, she landed a job as a waitress at Justin's Brasserie—a rather nice Frenchish Western pub. She honestly told the proprietor that she would be having a baby in six months, but she also promised that she would return six weeks later and work there for years.

After ten days on the job, Justin knew they had found a gem. She came early every day. She was a ray of sunshine for all their customers and rarely made a mistake on their bills. The actual place was rather cool. On weekends, they had live entertainment, usually easy rock, which simply added to the tips and the nightly enjoyment.

Fortunately, her baby girl was born hale and hearty six months later. Her name? Faith, which was chosen because mom Abby had some abiding belief that somehow, someway things would work out. Within four weeks, the mother had found a highly recommended young live-in au pair from Ecuador named Angela. Just to make sure, Abby stayed with the young woman for the first two weeks to make sure she knew where the groceries were stored and how to feed and change her daughter. After she checked out five references, she cemented the deal with Angela. However, naturally, she felt such sadness leaving her apartment and newborn daughter for her return to Justin's Brasserie.

The reaction at the pub buoyed her spirits. When she walked through the door, employees gave her a standing ovation. It made her cry, partly because of the separation from her little girl, Faith, and partly in gratitude that she actually had friends in Boulder, Colorado. That weekend, they had a tribute band at the restaurant that played the hits of the Jersey Boys. Big tips.

On Sunday Abby, Angela, and Faith visited the nearby parks where they could explore swing sets and jungle gyms. That was sort of the pattern for the next five years. Meanwhile, she had become the assistant manager at Justin's Brasserie, where she booked many of the weekend entertainment and created PR for the place.

Justin complimented her on her choice of weekend bands and the quality of the PR releases. "You have a talent for words," he told her. "Ever think of becoming a writer?"

"Every day," she answered with a smile. "But I am busy raising a young daughter—with some excellent help—and serving excellent cuisine."

Actually, she had thought about taking some writing classes, but when? Already she was working fifty hours a week and being as good a part-time mother as possible.

That routine was about to change. Always an attractive woman, Abby had a rare one-night stand with an out-of-town stud and became pregnant again. As soon as she found out the medical verdict, she contacted Angela, her au pair, and gave her a big raise to help care and commit to her growing family. Six months later there was another bundle of joy in the family. This time it was a boy. She named him Adam, the first man. Once again, she took six weeks off from the brasserie and helped on the home front.

It's insane to suggest that sixteen years just passed. There were soccer games, ski trips, and birthday parties for each kid, Angela, and Abby. Obviously, there were also difficult days. Kid disagreements. Arguments between mom and kids. The death of her father (who never spoke to her again after moving to Colorado).

There was also progress. Faith was now accepted at Colorado–Boulder. Adam was on a trajectory to become a math wiz at any college in America. Angela and Abby had become the best of friends. Meanwhile, Justin's Brasserie was now recognized by *Colorado Magazine* as the most wonderful place to spend a weekend night. According to the profile, most credit went to Abby Roades, who booked the best musical talent in all the Western states.

On one particular weekend two years later, when her young son Adam would attend Colorado State with a math scholarship and her daughter would become enrolled in grad school, they had a party at Justin's Brasserie, where there was a tribute video performance of the Beatles. Everyone danced. Everyone sang along. Everyone was happy.

The very next weekend, Abby enrolled in the local community college and studied writing. By that point she was in her late forties and began to believe that it may be too late for her. However, as her grades indicated, she didn't really need this affirmation. "You have a talent," "You have a gift," "You must pursue," the college profs advised her.

Two years later she published a book called *The Long and Winding Road.*

It was the story of the Beatles (and subliminally her tale as well). At the publication party at Justin's, more than 150 attended, with bravos from all.

Her kids were there. Faith gave a tribute to her mom. So did Adam. And so did Angela, who did so much to raise these young kids. That late night, all alone, she proudly realized she had accomplished something personal after all.

3

Curve Balls

My grandfather taught me to appreciate the unpredictable. "It's the only thing that makes each day interesting," I remember him saying. "Pray for curve balls. Otherwise, you just move through life in an automatic, straight line."

"But surprises are not always good," I innocently said. "One of my friends from school was in a bicycle accident last year. He got hurt."

"Sorry to hear that. Is he OK now?" my grandfather asked. Yep," I answered. "He just got a scratch."

"See! No real harm, Just a wake-up call from the unexpected to spice up his day," Gramps said with an A-OK gesture, and then he handed me a present. "Just to demonstrate the point, I got you a gift that we can play together."

I opened the bright package and discovered a plastic bat and a few white balls with holes in them. "Whiffle? Whiffle ball. What's that?" I asked, never having heard of the game.

"It's easy and fun," Grandpa said, and he walked me to the yard. He then threw some wicked curves my way, and I whiffed at every swing.

"Let me try to pitch," I asked. He showed me how to break the journey of the ball, took the bat, and motioned for me to show my best stuff. I think he may have hit two balls out of ten pitches. I had tons of giggles that first day, and we continued the practice at least once a week for the next several years. Along the way, he never lost the opportunity to remind me of the power of the unexpected.

It manifested itself in several ways. I remember when I was a sophomore in college and considering changing my major from English to journalism. My mom, dad, and most of my friends were against it. "Do it," my grandfather reassured me. "Everyone thinks you are a perfect English major, so what's the challenge? Surprise everyone. Work for a newspaper and tell stories." I did, and I have Gramps to thank for any success I have had in this field.

When I married my college sweetheart, Nellie, I even asked my grandfather to be in the wedding. He willingly accepted, and then he threw me another curve. Hi informed me that he was thinking of marrying again.

"Wow, that's a shock." I had never met my grandmother. She had died in her early thirties, and I only knew Grandpa Joe as a single widower. I didn't even know he went on dates. I just figured that his mission was to give me life lessons, which he still offered with aplomb. However, his fiancée Maura was very nice, and I was happy for Grandfather.

Given our changes in life, our games of whiffle ball were now a rare treat. However, I always valued the unpredictable in my life. My wife, Nellie, was now expecting our first baby, and I figured that qualified as a good surprise. When I called Grandpa Joe, he topped me. "Guess what? I've just been diagnosed with pancreatic cancer."

I almost dropped the phone. "No, that is not a funny curve ball," I responded haltingly.

"It's not even a curve ball," Grandpa corrected me. "It would be if I got this damn disease at your age or in my forties or even in my sixties. But I'm seventy-nine years old! This isn't such a shocker. It's the natural order. Now get your ass in here and see me. Maura has a gift for you.”

When I went to see him, he looked bad, and I was choked up. I told him I was going to name our firstborn after him—either Joseph or Josephine. When Maura entered the hospital room, she was all smiles and presented me a beautifully wrapped present.

“Give this to your little one,” Grandpa told me. “Make sure he or she understands the value of the unpredictable, and teach them how to throw a few curve balls of their own.”

It was the last time I saw Grandpa Joe. I still see Maura occasionally, and I invite her to the house now and then to watch me teach little Jo how to play whiffle ball and prevail over the curve balls of life. She’s only three, but she’s already pretty good at it.

4

Opiate Heaven

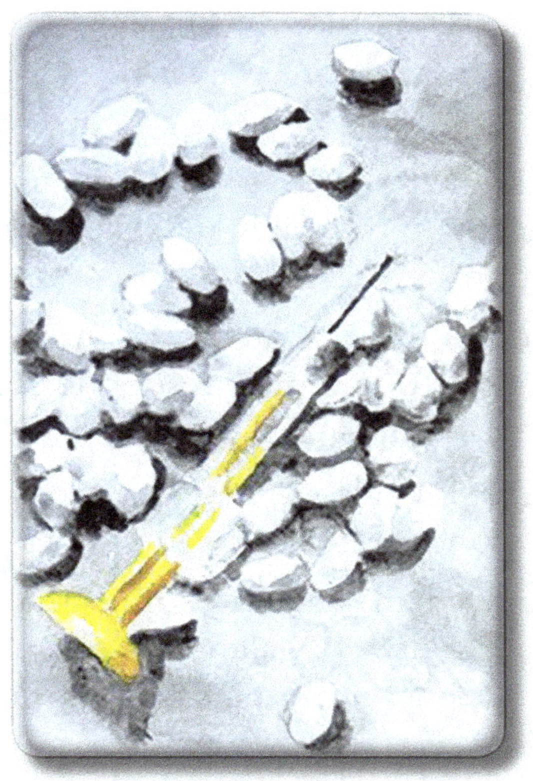

It's just human nature to try to alleviate pain. For that reason, when young Michael Quinn hurt his knee in his last high school football game, he limped off the field with his arms around two teammates and hoped that it would heal itself. It didn't. After twenty-four hours, his parents took him to the family doctor, who immediately demanded x- rays and an MRI. The verdict? A severely torn ACL, MCL, and meniscus. Ouch!

Dr. Jordan scheduled an operation within the next thirty-six hours, but he warned the young man and his parents that he would be in severe pain and most likely be unable to walk for weeks or even months.

"This should help," the doctor said, and he handed them a prescription for oxycodone. "Don't overdo it, but it's a miracle drug that affects the reward center of the brain and is able to block pain."

Actually, it did more than that. Like most opiates, it made Michael feel good.

Few people at the time (even doctors) knew the addictive dangers of this drug. True, they knew the effect, and for most people in pain, that relief was almost heaven-sent.

After his Christmas break, which the young man spent primarily in bed, Michael was finally able to hobble around on crutches—which tended to exacerbate the pain. He asked his doctor to re-up the oxycodone prescription.

"Maybe you should just switch to Advil or Tylenol," the doctor advised. "No, just one more prescription, Michael argued. "By then, I should be on a cane and in less pain."

The doctor acceded but also told Michael that this would be it. "While it does work wonders, I don't want you to get hooked on it."

Privately, the young man had to admit that he had begun to crave the drug. Its ability to alleviate all pain was downright miraculous. Almost of equal importance, it gave him peace and bit of a high.

By the time he was able to ditch the crutches and walk with a cane, he did his best to follow his doctor's advice. He did switch to Advil, which had some effect in alleviating the slow healing process of his knee operation, but it didn't give him that in-the-clouds feeling that oxycodone provided.

Sometime after he exhausted Dr. Jordan's final prescription, he was walking with a cane in the local park when a rather scuzzy guy approached him.

"You in pain?" the dealer asked.

"Yep."

"Out of oxycodone, Percocet, or morphine?"

"Yep."

"This stuff is better. It's twice as effective as morphine."

"What is it?"

"Heroin. Ten bucks. Give me twenty, I'll give you three needles just to get you started."

Michael looked around the park and saw no witnesses. So he reached into his pocket, found a twenty, and hoped this would give him the advantages of his prescription drug. It did. This "ohmm" escape continued for months since the dealer had given the young man his card when the student needed a new supply.

By September, the young man had enrolled in junior college and continued his habit, but Michael atypically flunked out his first semester because he had missed too many classes. As a fallback (and as a way to have some discretionary dollars), he joined the local parks department and helped rake leaves. Suspicious of this change in behavior, his mother checked his backpack one afternoon and found three needles.

"What are these?" his dad asked.

"Pain relief," he answered.

"Called?"

"Heroin."

"Oh my god," Marge, his mother, gasped.

Rather than get into a screaming match, Harry Quinn tried to reason with his son on the basis of love and sincere concern. He warned that heroin was a very addictive drug and that the long-term effects would not be good. They discussed the twists and turns of life that brought him to this danger—that is, how long, how often, how many people know, etc., etc. It was a fairly honest conversation. Michael admitted he did not want to be hooked on the drug.

Consequently, they created a plan of action. Within a month, Michael would take a two-week vacation from his new job, and his parents would find him a rehab center in hopes of kicking this habit.

They enrolled him in a center in Florida so he would be away from local influences. His only responsibility: "Listen to what they have to say, and take it to heart."

Michael tried. But it was not that easy. Even the best rehab center cannot enforce a change of behavior. It has to come from within. And the odds are against it.

Facts: From the 1970s through 2010, the amount of available opiates has increased perhaps fiftyfold. Ten times a day, Americans die of drug overdose (that's more than car crash deaths). Deaths from heroin increased 328 percent between 2010 and 2015.

Michael tried for a year. However, his brain and his psyche missed the thrill of the high. Consequently, after nine months, he again contacted his dealer and got back on the heroin program. Within a month, he was hooked. It was an escape. It felt so deserved. It felt so good.

A year later, he was reprimanded by the parks department for "no shows." He was also suspended for a month. In view of this, his parents checked his backpack again and found more needles. Consequently, they enrolled him again in another opiate retreat— this time in the tony Hamptons, where they could visit him every weekend and perhaps talk with counselors about his progress.

As they explained, "This may be a long struggle. We need to take this step- by-step. And he has to want it."

Within several weeks, he was back, but not all the way. He knew his parents suspected him (and loved him), but he wanted his own freedom. After a few months of being clean, he rented a storage space where he could store his needles.

After a few more months, he was found dead in the park where he had originally met his dealer. The autopsy confirmed that it was an overdose of heroin.

There are few experiences more gut-wrenching than preparing funeral arrangements for a twenty-two-year-old son. While fighting back tears all afternoon at the Wilson Funeral Parlor, Marge and

Harry Quinn picked out a casket and decided it should be open for viewing.

Hundreds of people came to the mortuary and paid their last respects. In fact, the line snaked around for about a half mile. Most didn't know that the young man was so afflicted, but wanted to share their condolences with the mom, dad, and sister. For almost all of us, it was strange to see such a young person surrounded by flowers, inside a mahogany casket. Most of us have become accustomed to seeing septuagenarians or octogenarians in such a prone restful position. But a twenty-two-year-old?

The service the next morning at Saint Agnes Catholic Church was equally packed with people just waiting to hear what Father Gallagher would have to say about a former altar boy who had overdosed on heroin. Fortunately, the men of the cloth have faith and a strong belief in the afterlife. At moments like this, they are at their best. With quiet sympathy, he stated that "people like Michael put up the good fight, but their pain becomes greater than they can manage." Also, "God invites us this morning to believe that there is life after death, that Michael now lives with God in heaven, that God will slowly heal the pain we feel at the loss of Michael."

He said more: "We rejoice today that Jesus, true to his promise, has taken Michael to the place he has prepared for him so he might be with his grandpas who have gone before him."

Marge Quinn sincerely hoped so, but she wasn't sure.

Inevitably, she felt much pain in the ensuing months and years.

However, she refused to take heroin to relieve it.

5

Khaki

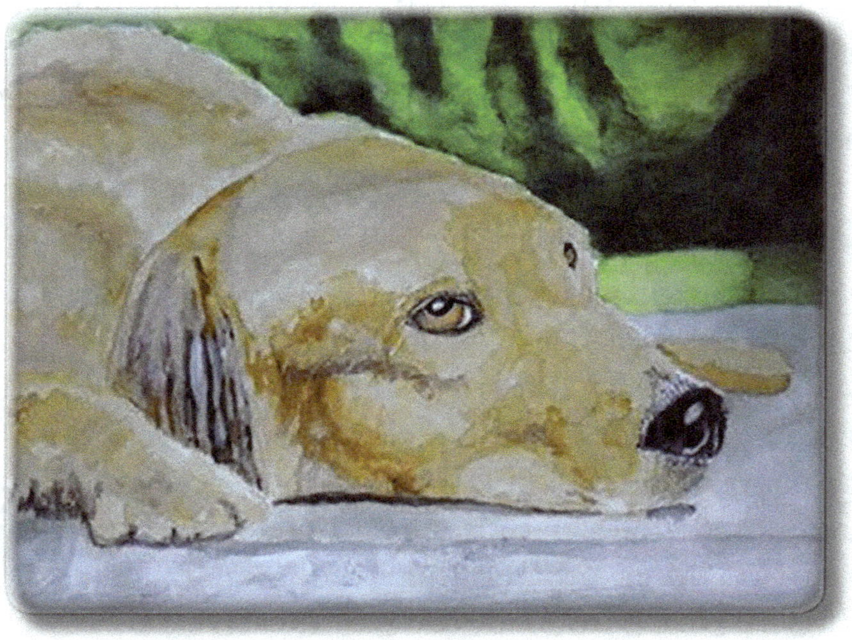

For fourteen years, I enjoyed the experience of living with the smartest dog in America. In some ways, she had an easy act to follow. After daily attempts to keep our beautiful Siberian husky in the yard, we finally gave up. I would drive around the neighborhood looking for this nomad, who would spot me in the car and then run in the opposite direction. Finally, we bestowed this wandering pet to my brother-in-law who lived on a mountain in Vermont. Plenty of room to roam.

However, we wanted another companion. At the time, I had five kids still in the house, and I always thought that it was a great childhood experience to have a loving pet. When my wife at the time visited a kennel with me and looked in the cages, it was love at first sight.

This particular golden had a knack of looking at you with doleful eyes that suggested, "Pick me, pick me, pick me." When the kennel guy opened the door, the young dog ran into my wife's arms and snuggled there. "I don't think I need to look any further," she said winking. So we paid the money, and Janice named her Khaki.

I am not a great dog trainer, but with Khaki, I didn't need to be. I sometimes kidded that I thought she spoke English. I remember explaining to her in the early days, "No shitting in the house. That's what the yard is for." To the best of my recollection, she never did. It was almost as if she understood.

"No barking at all the kids and parents that are walking in front of the house. Don't scare them. And don't go crazy on the mailman who is delivering packages. Do you understand?" With these instructions, I think she may have nodded yes.

"No sleeping in the bed." I know this little rule is often overlooked with those snooty itsy-bitsy toy dogs. But Khaki was a full-sized dog with lots of hair. Not for me. Don't misunderstand, she was an amazingly friendly dog who would ordinarily meet me at the front doors, shake her ass, and dip her head so I could give her a hug.

In exchange, I promised her that would treat her well, give her lots of hugs, and importantly, give her plenty of exercise. "Right, sons!" I called out. "We'll take turns. I'll give her a walk this afternoon, then Scott will tomorrow, then James, then Riley. Then Jack. Then me."

"Deal," they agreed.

And for years, that's exactly how it worked. The kids would take her to a nearby woods or park and walk freely with her (sometimes off the leash).

As the kids liked to brag, she would ordinarily walk in lockstep through the forest, never getting more than a few feet ahead or behind.

Normally, when we would play Ping-Pong or basketball in the backyard, she would sit on the sidelines and act as a cheerleader. Very, very occasionally, she would take a quick dip in the pool, but she could usually find a way up the ladder without ever tearing the liner.

Normally, at night, we would watch some stupid movie or sports event with Khaki at our feet on the carpet. I think she liked comedies the best. *Friends* was always fun, and as soon as the music would hit, I always thought she wanted to settle in for a good half hour of family time.

Tick-tock-tick-tock. Time marches on. One by one, the kids go off to college, only to return each summer. To my amazement, they were always greeted with licks and hugs from Khaki, almost as if they had never left.

In time I had her all to myself, and after a life of constant hubbub, I was thankful for that companionship. Each night, she would climb the stairs and sleep on the floor next to my bed. Each morning, I would wake around 6:00 a.m. to let her out to do her business.

Obviously, in time, the kids become independent and need to create their own lives as they should. At about this time, I lived in this big seven- bedroom home on an acre of land with one companion—a sweet Golden Retriever called Khaki. We would watch *Curb Your Enthusiasm* together, cheer for *American Idol* contestants, and occasionally plug in a movie. Each night, she would follow me up to the bedroom, where I would watch the evening cable news with her on the floor next to me.

But then something bad happened. Somehow, my favorite pet of all time began limping on her front foot. I thought maybe she had been attacked by a deer or a coyote, but according to my trusted vet, she was getting old and the foot was arthritic. Within six months, she truly did walk like a cripple and could no longer easily climb the stairs to sleep on the floor next to my bed. I ended up spending a little more time downstairs so we could at least be together.

But on one fateful night, I did hear her clumping up the stairs and sheepishly walk into my bedroom. In retrospect, I think it was almost as if she knew. When I woke up and carefully walked her down the flight of stairs, I was so happy to have another night in her company.

When I let her out, I watched her cautiously limp into the backyard while I prepared her morning meal. My gal Friday, Miriam, watched as we poured the dog food and the water.

"She stayed in your bedroom last night?" Miriam asked. "Yeah, she must be missing me," I boasted.

Unfortunately, I had an important meeting in lower Manhattan, and so I prepared for my journey.

"You think she's OK?" a perceptive Miriam asked. "She looks a little slow."

"Who wouldn't be? It's a long walk up and down a flight of stairs on three legs," I quipped.

And so, I got dressed for the event, and we fed our beloved Khaki for the last time. We decided it would be best to give her fresh air rather than make her struggle to get in and out of the house.

By the time I had travelled about twelve minutes, I got a call. It was Miriam. "Mr. John, I think she just died."

"No!"

"Seriously, she is still and not breathing."

"Oh my god, I will be right back."

Indeed, Miriam's instincts were right. When I got back home, I saw my brilliant, affectionate companion lying motionless on the patio, on her side. I sat there and looked at her at least a half hour, but I didn't really want to remember her this way. Thanks to my ex-wife's new husband, we wrapped her in a blanket and asked the vet to cremate her for a family ceremony.

We spread the ashes in a front yard garden, and all said a tearful prayer.

She was the best damn dog a guy could ever have. I miss her most days.

I have never replaced her and never will.

If I did and tried to explain it to Khaki, even in English, I don't think she would want that.

6

A Nightmarish Crash

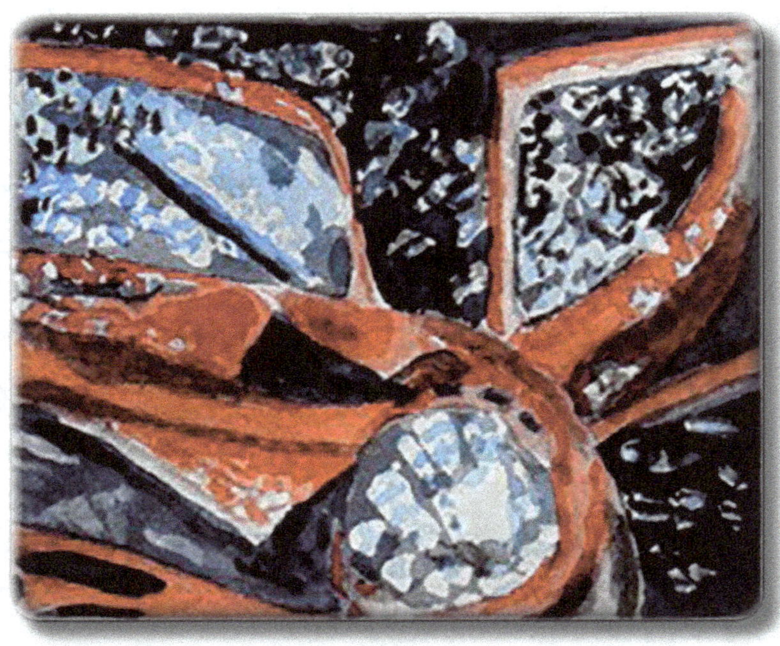

I had not witnessed such a bad accident since my dad was decapitated in 1990.

At the time, I was only fourteen. My mom and I were driving behind him as he drove his little Miata convertible down to the auto repair shop, and we proceeded to the grocery store. I recall that he had recently complained that the brakes were slipping and wanted to take it again to the dealership. Instead, he took it into the big rear end of a semi-truck. *Kaboom!* Over and out. But for me, the nightmares of that scene have lingered ever since.

The crash before me brought back all those painful memories.

Like most accidents, I couldn't see it coming. I was idling my beautiful red Mercedes in double-park mode right in front of Johnny's Pizzeria. A slice of their buffalo chicken variety was on my mind, maybe with an ice-cold fountain Coke. To be honest, I was tempted to duck in, grab the slice, and get on my way. But with my dumb luck, I

20

would probably get a stupid ticket for my little transgression, and it just wasn't worth the risk. So I waited for a parking spot to open up.

Finally, a middle-aged woman walked to her car, which was parked just to my right. Perfect! She turned on the ignition and then proceeded to put her change in her coin purse, readjust every mirror, and buckle her seat belt. Then she checked her hair and started applying lipstick. This delaying female really did piss me off, but I chose not to honk. Instead I put the gear in P and patiently waited.

The driver behind me was not so patient. I think it was teenager in a Toyota. He accelerated past my Mercedes on the left and rammed head-on into the massive cement truck that was barreling down the road in the opposite direction.

The teenager should not have been driving that fast. He should not have impatiently gunned his car past me on the double-yellow line. But that's the way accidents happen: Ten seconds ago, everything is A-OK. In the next instant—sometimes in the blink of an eye—people die.

I don't think either driver ever hit the brake. Given the difference in size and weight, the Toyota rebounded like a crushed rubber ball toward the left sidewalk, where a telephone pole was in the process of being erected.

The impact of the teenager's car knocked the pole off its temporary pilings, and then it started falling in my direction. The impending projectile seemed to approach me in slow motion. Unfortunately, my reflexes in moving my car to Drive were even slower. I struggled to disengage the gearshift, but I just couldn't. Maybe it was panic. I don't know.

The pole was now eight feet from completely crushing my roof. Then five feet. Then one foot.

And then I woke up.

Like a rocket, my body shot forward. Like every other night, I knew I would not easily get to sleep again.

In a cold sweat at 3:00 a.m., I poured myself a brandy and walked into the garage to see the glistening three-year-old Mercedes that had exactly ten miles on the odometer. As my shrink had told me, I would eventually need to overcome this phobia. The purchase was a brave step in the right direction. In time and with enough therapy, Dr. Kennett told me I would eventually gain enough courage to get behind the wheel and learn to drive the damn thing. Maybe someday. Just not now.

7

Bye-Bye, Bobby

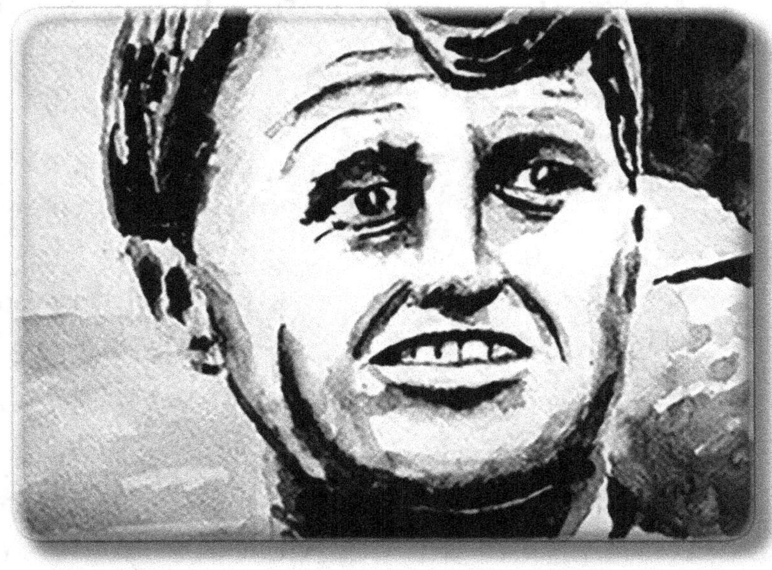

I was only thirteen years old at the time but had become a die-hard fan of Bobby Kennedy. While I admired JFK as a young boy, I had learned to respect Bobby as the real deal—an honest, semi reticent, not-so-slick guy who could represent the diversity of America's middle class like no one else and disagree with his brother about the war in Vietnam.

Unfortunately, I witnessed his assassination on TV, just after his victorious California primary. I was up all night, aghast at the tragedy; and for days, I walked around in a daze. The climax of that weekend was Teddy Kennedy's funeral eulogy at Saint Patrick's cathedral, where he quoted his murdered brother: "Some men see things as they are and wonder why. I dream things that never were and say 'Why not?'"

When I understood that the train would be coming through my local station of Glenholden, Pennsylvania, just past Sharon Hill. I wanted to be there. Unlike today's gatherings, it was not an organized PR event. People came spontaneously, simply out of grief, admiration, and tribute. By the time I walked to the tracks in anticipation of the estimated one thirty pass-by, there were probably thirty people there—of all ages and races. Many were holding handwritten signs that said "God Bless you, RFK," and "We Love You, Bobby."

Of course, the funeral train was delayed. Evidently, two million people lined the tracks from New York City to Washington, DC, where the presumably next president of the US would be buried in Arlington National Cemetery. Despite the one-hour delay, no one left the tracks.

If anything, dozens of more people joined the crowd. There were people in bathing suits and in suits and ties. Some kids had climbed the trees for a better view. There was even a wedding party who had decided to join the last goodbye.

At that age, I didn't have a wristwatch, but I guessed it was about an hour and half before we could see the train in the distance. It did slow down. As it did, a hush fell over the crowd. Some African American women fell in prayer. Men in suits made the sign of the cross. The group of bridesmaids tossed their flowers at the train. In the last car, I saw Ted Kennedy waving to the crowd and Ethel Kennedy, now pregnant with her eleventh child, throwing a kiss at me (and, I now assume, dozens of others).

The week definitely changed me. Given the recent assassination of Martin Luther King and the growing number of young Americans killed in Vietnam (one local kid was killed in the next week), it would be tempting to climb into my shell and become a hermit. Instead, I chose a path inspired by RFK.

I became involved. I went to college and then enrolled in the University of Virginia law school (where Bobby went). After years of court battles, I decided I could make a bigger difference running for Congress. Inexperienced as I was, I was elected in 1995.

It's a tough job, with lots of crazy Right or Left accusations, especially in view of our tribal politics. However, I persist. I have recently run for lieutenant governor and have fortunately been elected. For now, I am obsessed with the equal opportunity fairness of our legal system. Over the next decade, I hope to make a difference in bringing our different ethnic and religious cultures together.

As Bobby Kennedy said in one of his talks, "Why not?"

8

Concussed

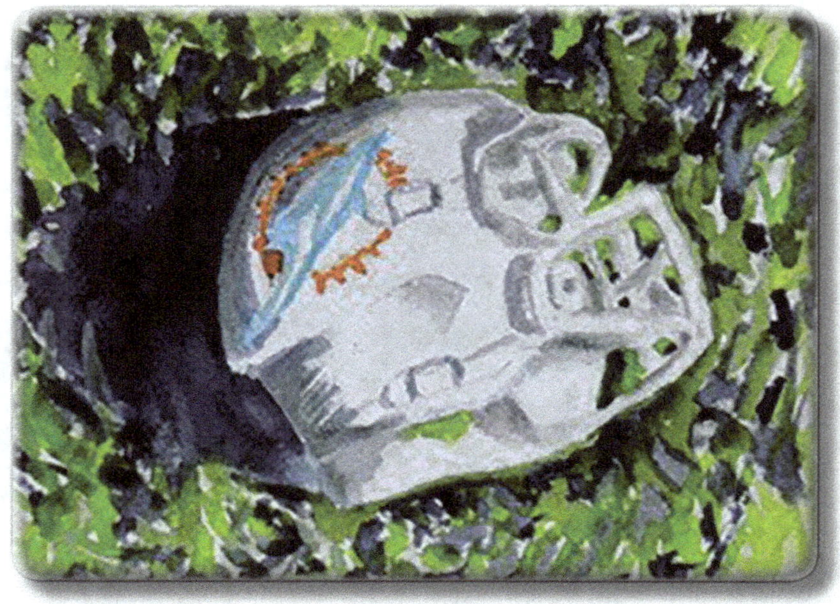

Young Edwardo Jr. asked his mom if he could play on the Orlando High School football team. Mom just looked in his eyes and tears filled her eyes. Given her life, it was a difficult and conflicting question. But as she thought about it, it wasn't that conflicting.

Let's go back twenty-eight years to the glory days.

It is without a doubt the most TV-watchable, advertising-friendly, and exciting sports contests on TV. Not surprisingly, it is also the most violent athletic competition every Sunday afternoon (and Monday and Thursday nights). Perhaps because of the heroic fame of the game, it attracted Edwardo "Moose" Cavanaugh in his high school years.

"Moose, the monster," was written in his high school yearbook, which chronicled his high school all-state record as the best tight end in Tennessee history. "The kid bangs ahead and mows over his opponents with crush-and-crunch enthusiasm," his local paper reported.

Not surprisingly, he was offered several college scholarships at prestigious schools. He eventually settled on the University of Florida, where he correctly figured he could gain headlines for his football prowess. In his third year, he was drafted by the Miami Dolphins and became a sensation in his first year. For those of you who are Dolphin fans, you undoubtedly know that he was an All-Pro five years in a row.

Along the way, he was carried off in a stretcher many times from helmet-to- helmet collisions. In Moose's heyday in the mid-nineties, nobody talked about the dangers of TBI (traumatic brain injury). Most particularly, the NFL largely ignored the issue until 2016, when Moose Cavanaugh started showing signs of dementia.

His wife, Dana, had noticed the symptoms several years after Moose retired from the NFL. At the otherwise spry age of forty-four, her husband suffered from imbalance, confusion, memory loss, malaise, early dementia, Alzheimer's disease, and several other symptoms. He was not the only one. Frank Gifford, Aaron Hernandez, Junior Seau, Bubba Smith, and Kenny Stabler were also similarly diagnosed.

So were 4,500 NFL players. They filed a class action suit signed to the NFL to acknowledge a connection between football and life-ending concussion. As a reluctant concession, the players gained a $765 million settlement for concussion research. In the process, it was discovered that 99 percent of deceased NFL players had diagnosed symptoms. (Actually, 110 of 111 former NFL players showed mental difficulties).

It's not always just a numbness of the brain. Many afflicted players like Aaron Hernandez and Junior Seau have been identified as murderers or suicide victims. Unfortunately, the only way to definitely diagnose the concussed illness is with a brain examination after death. In some incoherent way, Edwardo "Moose" Cavanaugh was not yet one of those victims. True, he had lost cognizance of life around him.

Doctors suggested he had early Alzheimer's disease. He often stumbled into bed, and his wife, Dana, did her best to make him comfortable.

Two days ago, young Edwardo asked his mother for her permission to sign the release form for him to play on the high school team. "Dad played and became famous," the son said. "I would like to follow in his footsteps."

"I don't want you to do that. It's dangerous," Mom responded. "So is walking down the street," Junior responded.

"Don't you have other ambitions?" Dana asked.

"I would also like to become a sportscaster," the kid said. "So do that," his mom responded enthusiastically.

Twenty-four hours later, young Edwardo Cavanaugh Jr. visited his dad in his bedroom. After extolling his dear father's career and life-path, he asked the man for advice.

After a few minutes, the Moose responded. "Who's Eddie?" the man asked in a daze, and he searched around the room.

His young son reached across and grabbed his father's hand. The kid closed his eyes and asked his mother to excuse him for some time with his barely lucid father.

Within three weeks, Edwardo "Moose" Kavanaugh Jr. enrolled in the University of Missouri Journalism School and eventually became a play-by- play sports broadcaster for the NFL. Since that day, more and more NFL players have signed a collective grievance against the NFL for loss of memory via concussions on the field. Millions of dollars have been earmarked for the afflicted, but for anyone who has lost a husband, dad, or friend, it is not nearly enough.

Very Old Stars

Fittingly, the seventy-year-old movie theater on Fourth Street was called the Golden Standard. In its heyday in the midtwentieth century, it premiered such classics as *Gone with the Wind*, *Sunset Boulevard*, and *Casablanca*. That was a long time ago. That was when the citizens of Louisville would dress up on dates to see the stars of the silver screen and lose themselves for a few hours in the celluloid magic of the movies.

As was common in many inner-city movie palaces, it became a rather threadbare showcase for black exploitation films in the early 1990s. After a few years of dwindling audiences, this once-glittering cinema was shuttered.

That's when Bernard Harris entered the picture. He had always been a fan of showbiz, but he was an even bigger fan of the real estate biz, especially when he could secure a sweet deal. This particular transaction was honey- dipped sugar.

From his friends in the government, he learned that the Golden Standard would soon be designated a historical landmark. As such, it provided rather generous dollars-and-cents advantages—the place qualified for a 20 percent tax offset on all rehabilitations, local property tax reductions, and charitable deductions on federal returns (since the theater had a history in the arts).

Add to that the fact that the thousands of young loft-loving, college-educated Louisvillians wanted to reclaim the inner city for their urban lifestyle, and you have the perfect equation for a famous business.

Let's not race past that second last word in the previous sentence. While Mr. Harrison did not personally crave fame, he did appreciate that incandescent allure from Hollywood. Consequently, he chose to lionize those stars in the newly rehabbed Golden Standard Cinema. While he never promised the landmark folks that he would only show classic films, it was always his intention. A big part of this was personal taste. He hated the "car chase, exploding buildings, and CGI" theory of moviemaking so prevalent today. A bigger part of his screenings had to do with an evangelical sense of mission. "If only people would rediscover these film classics and inspirational stars, the world would be a better place," he promised the *Louisville Courier* when the movie palace was again opened.

"If you build it, they will come," James Earl Jones announced in the mystical *Field of Dreams*. However, the citizens did not come to the black-and-white classics at the Golden Standard. In 2012, James Cagney, Dorothy Lamour, and Joan Crawford had little built-in box office appeal.

An ordinary man might decide to pocket the profit and simply screen *Wedding Crashers* V. Instead, Bernard Harrison somehow believed in the gestalt of the classic movie experience. Perhaps, he told his kids, it was time for him to be as creative as the studio chiefs. But how to do so and attract the weary workers of Louisville? For starters, he combined genres on each weekend—Mafia movies, a Western weekend, a Bogart festival, a "Fall in Love with Tracy and Hepburn" gala, an "Isn't Cary Grant Cool?" celebration. This started to attract an audience.

Then he added cuisine to the offering. Instead of gummy bears, whoppers and Reese's pieces, he offered fettuccine Alfredo and calamari fritti for the Mafia movies. The Western weekend featured pulled-pork sandwiches. The "Isn't Cary Grant Cool?" celebration was accompanied with ice cream sandwiches, gelato, and flan. Local chefs began to compete for star-studded evenings. As you might know from your own local community, this sort of integrated entertainment became *de rigueur* among classic movie theaters.

Last June, Bernard Harrison passed away in peace at the age of eighty-two. At the time, the *Louisville Courier* did a two-column obit about his contributions to the community. This write-up thrilled his surviving sons and daughter. What thrilled them even more was the fact that today they just learned that, given his unique contribution to Hollywood legends, Bernard would be honored with a star on the Hollywood Walk of Fame next year. Quite appropriately, he will be forever seen between Mae West and Clark Gable.

If you're ever in the neighborhood, "Frankly my dear, come up and see him sometime."

The Worm Who Wished He Could Fly

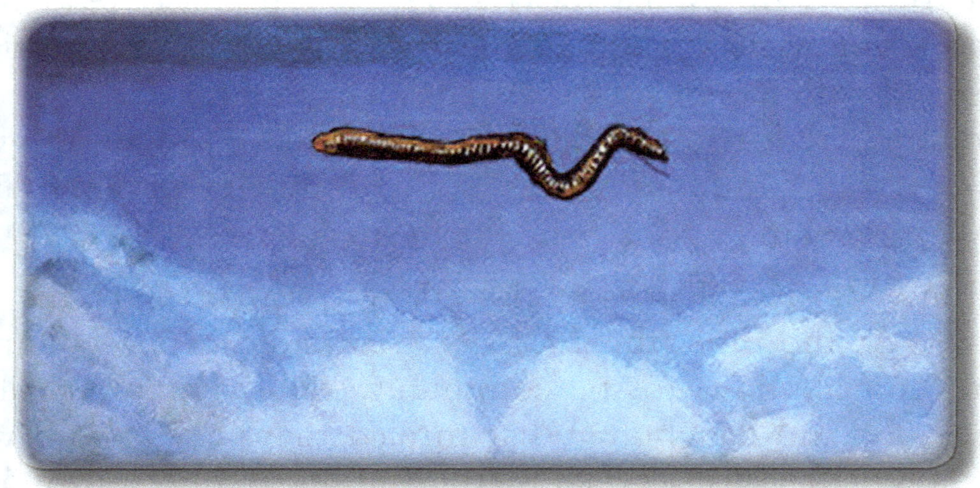

Once there was a worm who wanted to be more than a worm. His name was Joe. In appearance he was just an ordinary earthworm. He was long, brown, and slimy. And when he moved, he moved like an ordinary earthworm—very, very slowly.

I wish I were fast, he dreamed. It seemed like such a marvelous idea to zoom across the land and swim at superfast speeds. But, alas, every attempt proved fruitless. He squirmed over to his favorite maple tree and watched the clouds for inspiration. He also watched the birds and the bees and the butterflies. Then he suddenly perked up.

Wait, he said to himself. If *all those animals can fly, why can't* I? He thought of the thrill of sliding through space. Yes! He turned his body into a circle so he could float like a Frisbee. He formed a V with his body so he could sail like a boomerang. But nothing worked.

Then one day he met a butterfly named Cecily. She was beautiful. She was graceful. She was wonderful. Joe and Cecily became good friends. You might even call them lovers. They played and laughed together every day.

And while they were visually mismatched, they were very happy.

One day, Joe asked Cecily to teach him to fly.

"Why?" she asked.

"So I can move faster. I want to move as fast as you."

"Why?" she asked. "The sky isn't all it's cracked up to be. It's windy. It's cold. It's crowded."

"Teach me how," he persisted. "What do I need?"

"Wings," she eventually answered. "Without them, it's impossible to fly.'

"Then I've got to get wings." Joe turned around to see his slick wingless back.

"Hmmm. There has to be another way."

All through the summer months, he tried to come up with an ingenious plan.

As the autumn leaves began to fall, one came to him. "Cecily! Cecily! I figured out a way I can get wings!"

The butterfly just shook her head. "No, Joe. It isn't natural. Just be you. Warm, sensitive, caring Joe."

But the worm was obsessed. "I can use the sap from the tree and make leaf wings." Joe began to rub his back on the base of his favorite tree and lathered it with the sticky stuff. He then affixed a large yellow maple leaf on his skinny back. Unfortunately, there was not enough room for another. "One wing it is. I'll use it as a sail and fly the skies with you."

But every time Joe tried to catch the wind, he simply flipped over. "Teach me how," Joe pleaded.

"Joe, it's too windy and too cold." "Teach me how," Joe insisted.

Reluctantly, Cecily lifter her wings up, caught the wind, and went up and up and up. *What a lovely sight*, Joe thought.

Joe watched her flitter around and was getting worried. Given the howling wind, she was flying helter-skelter right toward his favorite maple tree.

"Come back," Joe cried, and then he turned away. Silently, he began to squirm toward the tree. When he reached the midpoint, he stopped.

He reached for Cecily, wrapped her in his tail, and carried the lifeless body all the way down. It was the slowest, most awful trip of his life.

He then rubbed his body until he tore his leaf wing off. He carried it over to Cecily and laid it on top of her. He said a prayer and trudged into the howling wind.

Joe wasn't exactly sure where he wanted to go. But he knew one thing. He wasn't in any hurry to get there. Not anymore.

Oh, My Papa

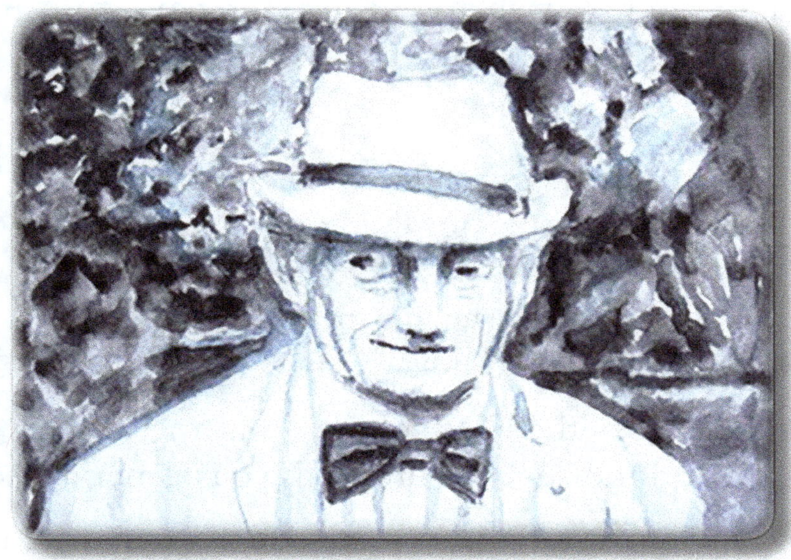

The gaunt man walked into the Todd-Hewitt funeral home with a bag full of memorabilia. "May I speak with one of the funeral directors," he asked.

"Certainly," the receptionist quietly answered, accustomed to meeting people in their hour of grief.

Within a few minutes, a middle-aged gentleman in a dark-gray suit came to the front desk and introduced himself. "My name is Jeffrey Todd. How can I help you?"

"My name is Billy Chastain, and I would like to arrange and orchestrate my upcoming funeral."

"Orchestrate?" the funeral director asked.

"Well, I wouldn't need a full orchestra," Billy quipped. "But I would like it to be somewhat theatrical."

After a pause, Mr. Todd asked the visitor if he wouldn't mind following him into his office. Once inside, he pulled out a chair across the desk and asked the man to share his thoughts. "Talk to me," the funeral director prompted.

"I have cancer and will probably be gone in three or four months. By then, I will look like a skeleton of myself. You won't even recognize me. Certainly none of my five kids will. I will not want an open casket. However, I wish my visitors to have fond memories of me and, perhaps, an inspiration for their own days ahead."

"What do you have in mind?"

"A video of me … with my kids … through the years. A friend of mine in Hollywood does this for her deceased friends with a music track. Most of her buddies die of AIDS, and she creates a chronicle of their lives together. In her case, it's mostly just a song. I thought it might be more impactful to do it as a mini movie."

As Billy looked across the desk, he saw that the funeral director was taking notes. "Ever done such a thing?" the customer asked.

"This would be a first," Mr. Todd soberly answered. "We have accommodated slide shows and specified music, but we have not yet previewed a mini movie in one of our parlors."

"Do you have a good sound system in your parlors?" Billy asked. "Well, it's not a nightclub," Mr. Todd answered. "But we could upgrade the system to enhance the sound. By the way, what's the song you have in mind?"

"It's an old song by Eddie Fisher called, 'Oh, My Papa.' Wanna hear it?" "No, no, no," the funeral director demurred. "Perhaps when we get a little closer to the actual event. Would you like to view caskets and pick out a favorite? Is there a next of kin that will be handling the details of this arrangement? At the risk of sounding monetary, who should I bill?"

"I will pay in advance," Billy answered, and he brought out a check for more than enough.

"Wow," Mr. Todd remarked. "This is probably the most unusual funeral arrangement I have ever had. But I will do my best to make it special. And I will upgrade our sound system for the event. Perhaps the cancer doctors will reverse their diagnosis, and you will be with us for another year or two or three. Who knows?"

"I already know," the thin, jaundiced Billy answered. He shook hands with the funeral director and waved goodbye.

Exactly three months and one week later, the body of Billy Chastain was in parlor B in a closed casket. There were probably one hundred visitors, townspeople, and relatives at the wake. All of Billy's five children were there to greet those who had come to offer their condolences.

At eight thirty, Jeffrey Todd introduced himself.

"I stand before you in behalf of Mr. Billy Chastain, who visited me three months ago. He had brought in a bag of pictures of his life in this community and asked me to help him create a tribute to all of you in this room who made his life special. Dim the lights," he called out to his assistant in the back room.

Within a few seconds, the lights slowly dimmed, and the music began to play. Over this track, they saw Billy as a young man with young kids. Then as a baseball coach. Then on vacations with his children. Then as the father of the bride. And then … and then … and then.

By the time the music and the video ended, there was not a dry eye in the house. It was an unusually emotional moment, even for a mortician. All the people in parlor B were hugging each other and wanted to stay longer.

In the aftermath of this reaction, Jeffrey Todd retreated to his office, and lit a rare celebratory cigar. As he puffed on the stogie, he reflected on the day and vowed to add video *remembrance* to his list of offerings to new customers.

One More Voice

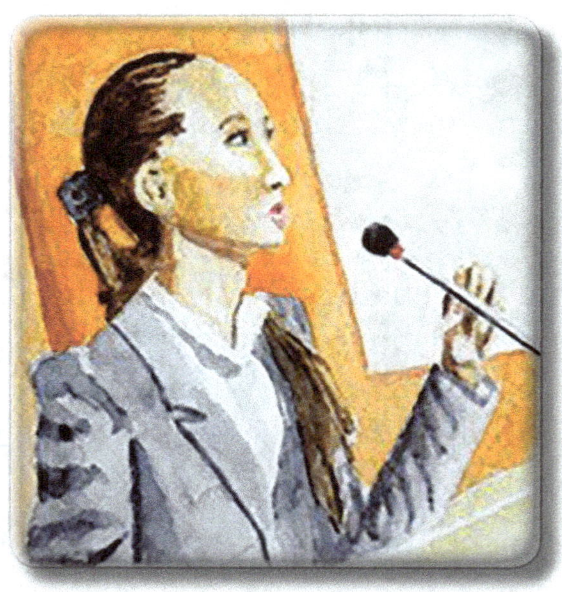

She was inspired by the courage of teenager who protested the deaths of seventeen classmates (and fourteen wounded) at Marjory Stoneman Douglas High School in the rather nice neighborhood of Parkland, Florida.

Fortunately, Linda Gormley had not lost her daughter on that February 14. However, little Mara was traumatized on the day of the massacre. She had known many of the students who were gunned down that day. Some were freshmen. Some were seniors. Some were gym teachers. For weeks, she had wakes and funerals to attend. For months, she had nightmares.

As anyone who lives in America knows, this was not an isolated incident. Last year alone, 2,700 students were shot and killed in various schools across this nation. Fourteen thousand five hundred were shot and injured. And still the students in the United States mourn and live in fear of the next slaughter, which could occur just weeks from now (statistics indicate that these unsuspected blasts occur every few weeks in America).

Not surprisingly, the students have begun to express their deep concerns about this latest incident. A young man named David Hogg from Parkland has actually campaigned in several states, imploring citizens and legislators to take action. He organized "March for Our Lives," in Washington, DC, and eight hundred other cities. He proposes universal background checks (even today, you can buy an assault weapon A-18 without a background check). He organized a "die-in" at Publix stores for twelve minutes to dramatize the deaths. He will speak on behalf of his lost friends and students almost anywhere.

Linda heard him in Sarasota. She was moved and somewhat embarrassed that she had not become more active before the young man's lecture. After all, she had been sympathetic with the movement, especially after Sandy Hook.

She decided it was no longer honorable to sit on the sidelines and become a head-in-the-sand ostrich, as more students would inevitably be killed. In her heart, she believed that government reform was probably the true solution.

After hemming and hawing for several weeks, she decided to announce her candidacy for the US House of Representatives. As the mother of a Parkland survivor, she created quite a publicity burst, especially when it was combined with her five-year term on the school board, her experience with Florida environmental issues, and her intention to protect senior citizens' social security benefit.

Yes, of course, the gun-toting lobby did oppose her. Living in an NRA state, she fully understood that she would be undercut with a multimillion- dollar budget of lobbying money.

However, she did have some advantages. For one thing, as a school board mother, she was able to have many town hall meetings on school grounds.

Often, her speeches would address large crowds and attract pro-gun protesters just outside the gatherings. This contretemps tended to attract national TV cameras, and the reportage was generally not flattering to the NRA, especially in view of the weeping parents of seventeen dead victims in Parkland. The contrast of tears and NRA shouts tended to galvanize local voters and attract many national politicians to the local Florida race, including Barack Obama, Chuck Schumer, Representative Julian Castro, and Kamala Harris from California.

Each of these visits tended to boost Linda Gormley's standings in the polls.

Two days before the election, student activist David Hogg appeared at one her rallies and attracted more than ten thousand people. As he told the crowd, he was proud of Ms. Gormley, and it had restored his faith in America. "I have done my best to raise awareness of this scourge, but it can't all come from students. It also has to come from grown-ups … and from voters. Don't be lazy. Don't stay at home. Vote. I can tell you, if the students at Parkland were old enough to vote, they would. We only ask the same from you."

Linda Gormley thanked him and guaranteed the crowd that she would work her butt off to make gun laws more sane, but also do her best for local issues that affected the constituency of Parkland.

At the end of her address, the local high school band played "God Bless America," which was filmed and telecast by all national networks, as the NRA signs offered messages of "Don't take our guns away," "Support the Second Amendment," and "Don't restrict freedom."

Twenty-four hours later, the voting day brought out record crowds. In this historically Republican district (Trump carried it by twenty-three points in 2016), CNN and MSNBC dubbed it "too close to call" even four hours after the polls had closed.

Like many Americans, I assume young David Hogg and his classmates were glued to the TV results. As a simpatico soul, so was Linda. At 2:00 p.m. only two hundred votes separated her from her gun-toting opponent. She advised her crowd to get some sleep. "We won't know for several days, and there may a recount … either way." She warned.

I have faith that it will end up well. But I must now sleep. If she wins, I promise to support her agenda. If she loses, I promise to support her resistance.

13

Just an Ordinary Hero

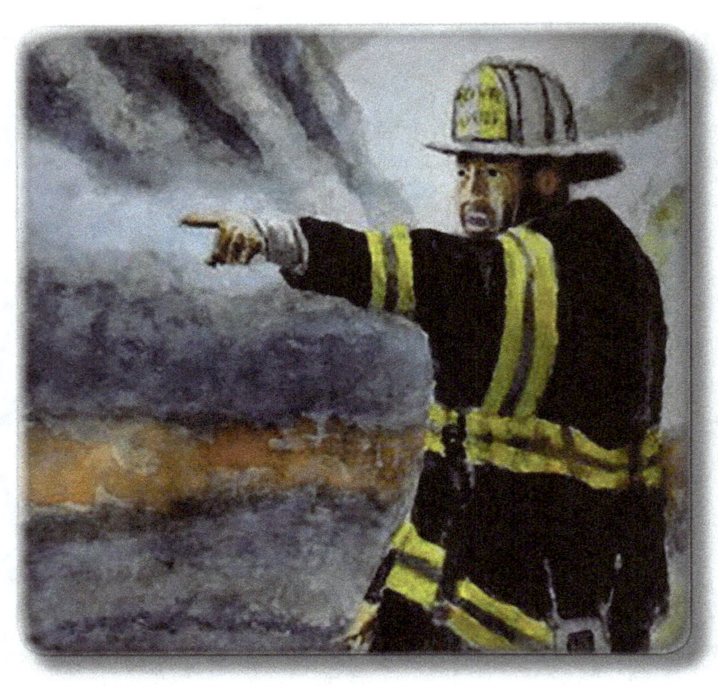

He doesn't look like Redford.

And he cannot dunk a ball.

Hell, he doesn't have a talk show,

Or a book that tells all.

He doesn't own a mansion,

And he wouldn't if he could.

He just goes about the job all through the day and night

He's so good.

— "Ordinary Hero," song by Doug Katsaros and John Nieman

The balmy beautiful morning of 9/11 changed things forever for New York City and probably for the world. There was mayhem down in lower Manhattan. At first people thought it was an accidental crash into the World Trade Center, perhaps from a private plane. However, within a half hour, when the second airplane crashed into the second tower, everyone knew this was no accident.

Soon, a different airliner crashed into the Pentagon, and then (given the teamwork of passengers in Pennsylvania) another crash occurred over farmland.

"By God, this is an attack," newscasters announced. "Clearly, hundreds of innocent Americans have been killed."

The carnage had only begun. Within minutes, NYPD personnel and firefighters from dozens of borough firehouses descended on the trade center towers without a second thought.

Before our eyes, we watched the two towers collapse upon each other, killing thousands more. There were firefighters and police officers in the buildings that crushed all life.

This is the story of one of them. Yes, of course, he had a name and a history. He had a wife and a family and a neighborhood home. However, he was not about fame or fortune. Perhaps that's why he became a firefighter.

Just to serve.

Consequently, I will honor that anonymity and just do my best to tell the story of his meaningful life and heroic death.

By the time his fire truck arrived at Tower 2, he could see that this was a desperate situation. Rather than endure the flames, many of the employees in the tower simply accepted suicide as the better option than incineration. Consequently, they were jumping out of windows.

"Get in there," he called to his band of brothers. "It's at least on the eightieth floor. Hustle, hustle. Grab a gas mask and hustle. I will be right behind you."

That had always been the code of this particular firefighter. He wouldn't think of sending his staff into harm's way and sitting on the sidelines in some relative safety. No, instead of spending time on his walkie-talkie, he followed his teammates up the staircases.

Before he and his buddies could reach the thirtieth floor, the tower collapsed.

The horror of that scene was miserably jarring for everyone to see, especially since it was repeated on all the networks every five minutes for days. Obviously, it was even more painful for family members who continued to hold out hope that someone would find their loved ones. Like many other spouses, our hero's wife visited the scene for four straight days. It was worse than she thought. The rubble all around her was stomach-wrenching. Even so, she brought a picture of her dear hubby to put on the wall in hopes that someone might miraculously find him.

They didn't. Like 383 valiant firefighters and 3,000 tenants, he was gone. On her last day in the ruins, she stood in front of her husband's photo for a least an hour, trembling with tears. Finally, she gave the longest kiss to the picture and put the photo in her purse. At the time, she couldn't imagine she would ever return to the scene of the crime. In fact, it took more than a decade, when the memorial opened. After all those years, she still felt so close to her long lost husband.

Just an ordinary hero.

Lives just down the way.

Hugged his wife when she lets him know there's another one coming any day

Gets a call from ground zero.

But before he goes, one kiss should last forever, We're gonna miss him so.

He didn't have to do.

Don't know how he was made that way.

But someone out there is thankful that he saved a life today.

Just an ordinary hero.

And a faithful friend.

If he could he'd still be out there and do it all again. And do it all again.

14

Pulling the Plug

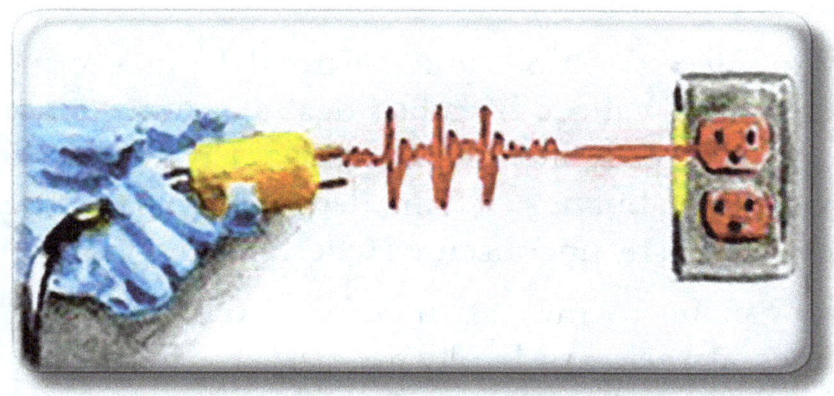

I was not appointed God on this earth. However, I was appointed son of a great dad who had coached my baseball teams, would talk to any stranger, worked around the clock to keep our small track home from going into foreclosure, and encouraged me to go to church every Sunday.

I always felt I owed my parents so much. My mom taught to me to draw and paint at the kitchen table; my dad loved words and crosswords puzzles, and he gained me a job as a movie and theater critic at his neighborhood newspaper. It didn't pay much—the price of a movie ticket or a Muny Opera free seat, but it did give me a byline in the *Florissant Reporter* and the itch to put my thoughts and emotions into the written word.

After college, I wished to pursue my own dreams and become an actor in New York. I remember my dad supporting that fantasy without so much as a whimper. He never groused—perhaps because he too was born in a different city (Cincinnati) and inherently believed in the American dream. "Only here can you pursue what you really want to be."

Perhaps as a WWII vet at Normandy, my dad cherished our unique freedoms. At the risk of getting political, I wish more people did today.

As a New Yorker now, I would still visit my home town of Saint Louis about once a year. I had many friends there from high school and college— and more importantly, my parents lived there and missed me.

On one trip a few decades ago, I learned from my mom that my father had esophageal cancer. It's a bad deal. It's almost always fatal. Of course, I was not ready to say goodbye. I went back every few months to visit him, but I saw him degenerate into a near skeleton and, ultimately, be mostly unconscious when I would visit.

I remember talking to my parish priest and asking him to visit my dad many times a week. As I told the pastor, "I have tried to speak with him. But I think he needs a higher order to help him pass in peace." According to my mom, the priest came three times a week. Consequently, I began contributing again to the church.

On my last several visits to Saint Louis, my dad was in the hospital and in severe pain. Not surprisingly, my mother was distraught. My sister would visit as often as she could but was also busy raising a family of young children. I remember my last visit in the hospital. The doctor motioned that he would like to have a private conversation with me, so we went out into the hall. "He's not getting better and he's not going to get better. It's more pain and more IV's every day. Got any thoughts?"

I did. But somehow I didn't think the decision would be on my shoulders. I simply looked back into the hospital room where my once vital father now lay in severe pain.

I still don't know if this is legal, but the doctor asked me if I wanted him kept alive with extraordinary medical means. I always knew my dad to be an independent soul and couldn't imagine he would like to be on unconscious life support. Without much hesitation, I think I remember telling the doc to "pull the plug."

I remember leaving the hospital shortly after that statement and walking around the block for forty-five minutes. Within twenty-four hours, my father passed in peace. I think the priest even came later that night to give him his last rights.

Of course, the next months and years were difficult. I had to pick out a casket and arrange funeral arrangements with my mother. However, I never regretted my decision.

It's a tough choice, but I sincerely hope that if I am ever in a similar dire situation, at least one of my kids will have the courage to say, "Pull the plug."

15

The Bucket List

On his sixty-fifth birthday, Bernard Carey did two significant things. During the day, he attended the funeral mass of his best friend, Louis, who had suddenly died of a heart attack just two days ago. Losing any dear friend is a devastating event, but the over-and-out of a decades-long buddy-buddy relationship was particularly searing for Bernard. After long marriages that ended in the same year and a similar experience of kids who moved out of town and created their own lives, Bernard and Louis found themselves in similar situations. Consequently, they tried to create their own day-to-day fun. It normally included a lunch or two every week, sometimes a day at the racetrack, and an occasional movie. Nothing spectacular.

That very thought is what suddenly haunted Bernard. *Should we have done bigger things? he asked himself. Who knew he would die so immediately before he could express his thoughts and regrets or finish his uncompleted tasks?*

That question prompted Bernard to pull out a blank piece of paper and begin filling out his to-do list on the evening of his sixty-fifth birthday. Of course, there were things like "keep contact with the kids," "save a few more dollars," and "try to be more optimistic." Then he pulled out a different sheet of paper and titled it "My Bucket List." It included more exotic adventures, like skydiving, visiting the Taj Mahal, and Machu Picchu, and taking the next random flight to anywhere.

After completing his personal bucket list, he went to JFK International Airport and booked the next available flight to Iceland, where he viewed the northern lights and swam in the hot springs of the Blue Lagoon.

The next week, he enrolled in an adult evening class to learn French (his personal bucket list, number 12: "learn a foreign language"). After eighteen months of lessons, he felt confident enough to visit Montreal and not rely on his native English language. What a thrill!

In the interim, he visited NYC New Year's fireworks display despite years of resisting this extravaganza and the associated traffic jam, and he had to admit he enjoyed it. He had vowed to help a total stranger and did so at least once a week with pride. In Ireland, he bought a drink for everyone at the bar, and he felt magnanimous in doing so.

Ultimately, he did take tango lessons and met a woman of his age. Within months, he felt he had found the new love of his life. Her name was Jenny. In the last several years, they had become an amazing couple. They cooked together and dined together. They went to the racetrack. At least once a week, they tangoed together.

On a quiet evening in his library, Bernard was going through his files and decided to review his bucket list. To his satisfaction, he had completed most of the missions he created for himself eight years ago.

In the back recesses of his brain, he admitted that it would be a good time to die. And yet he didn't want to. On the second last line of his original bucket list, he had hoped to "find the true love of your live." He had found Jenny.

And that exploration of everyday adventures had energized him.

Instead of dealing with the afterlife, Bernard moved to his treadmill in the next room and felt invigorated. After a twenty-five-minute run, he sat at his desk and pulled out another blank sheet of paper.

It was titled "My next bucket list." It included African safaris, Moscow, and playing golf at Saint Andrew's in Scotland.

As he looked at his new bucket list, he hoped that his golf dream could hopefully be completed with his dear Jenny.

16

The Boat Bag

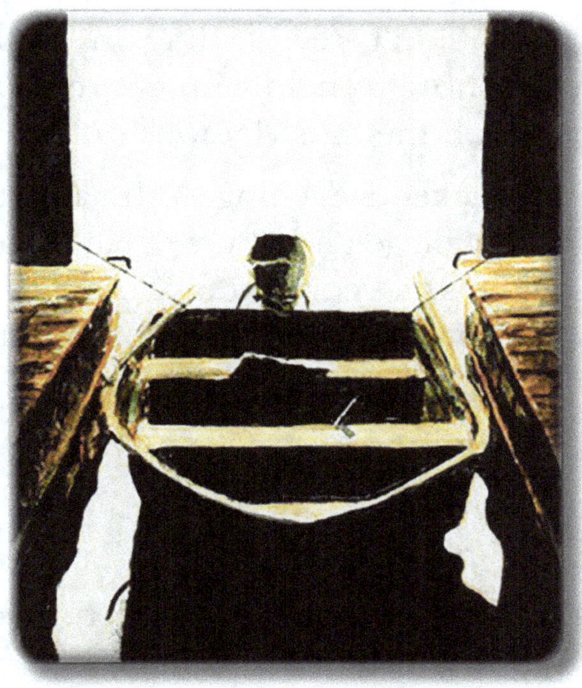

Carolyn Banks always loved the water. Consequently, it was fortunate that she lived in Sag Harbor, perhaps the premier boating community on the northern coast of Long Island. What was not fortunate was that she had been unhappily married for two dozen years to George Banks, who had a nasty habit of bragging that he was the best sailor in the area and would often continue his boastful self-aggrandizements at the local bars after a day at sea.

In the early years of their marriage, Carolyn would occasionally play second mate, help to flip the jib, and secure the lines after "coming about."

After a few years of her husband's braggadocio evenings about his superlative sailing talents (with nary a mention of his sailing partner), Carolyn began to tire of her husband's self-constructed pedestal.

After five years of this tiresome rigmarole, she was down to sailing once a month with her husband George. On the other eleven weekend days, Captain Banks recruited neighbors and friends to sail on the forty-six-foot Jeanneau Sun Odyssey, which he had named *Magnifico*, in anticipation of his prowess tacking and anticipating wind changes. Sometimes when he couldn't recruit known souls, he would hire young teenagers on the shore to help with chores on the boat and gain the privilege of sailing with the most famous sailor in Sag Harbor.

On many of these weekend evenings, Mr. and Mrs. Banks would visit the hot spots in the village and enjoy small plates and cocktails, as was the custom in this upscale community. Inevitably, they would run into people that they knew from this small community.

"George, I hear you are doing well on the boat," one well-wisher named Nancy Grimes admitted.

"Yes, I have been winning a lot of races, but that's only to be expected, given the fact that …"

Nancy Grimes interrupted the egotist and turned her attention to Carolyn.

"But, Carolyn, I rarely see you on the docks. If you ever care to go out on a stupid sail to nowhere—just an escapist afternoon—give me a call. It might be fun."

Fun? That was a concept she had almost forgotten about life on the water. The comment, of course, did not sit well with Carolyn's husband. Later that night, he scoffed at the offer and asked, "What's the point?" Not surprisingly, Carolyn just shook her head and endured another night with no sex.

In the ensuing seven years, George sailed every weekend day with hired crews and won six regattas. (He complained that his loss six years ago was way too close to call and disputed the decision.) In those same years, Carolyn sailed with Nancy about once a month, usually on a last-minute notice.

Last year, Nancy met a new man who liked to sail. For several months, Carolyn continued her intermittent routine with her sailing compadre, but she fully recognized that those days were numbered, especially since her gal friend had found a main squeeze at that late point in life.

Six months ago, her husband George suffered a massive heart attack and died within a few hours. As much as she hated to admit it, Carolyn did not shed a tear but did hold court at the funeral parlor for her kids and the many visitors who droned on about his sailing expertise. As usual, there was little info about his twenty-three-year marriage to Carolyn.

It was a stunning, life-changing event.

In the next year, she sold that sailing boat called Magnifico for $260,000.

She immediately created a trust fund in that amount for her two children.

She also bought a small rowboat on the harbor for an occasional reacquaintance with the water.

Alone in the boat with a smile on her face, it was a one-time event.

On Saturday morning, the boat was found floating in the water with no sign of a survivor. The Coast Guard marked the spot and pulled the boat into the Sag Harbor boatyard. The military folks went back to the site with deep-sea divers and tried to ascertain if someone was lost at sea.

There was no evidence of this.

On the next morning, they opened the bag on the boat. The handwritten message read as such:

I am where I wish to be. At sea. At peace. All by myself.

X, Carolyn

17

Lifeguarding Very Occasionally

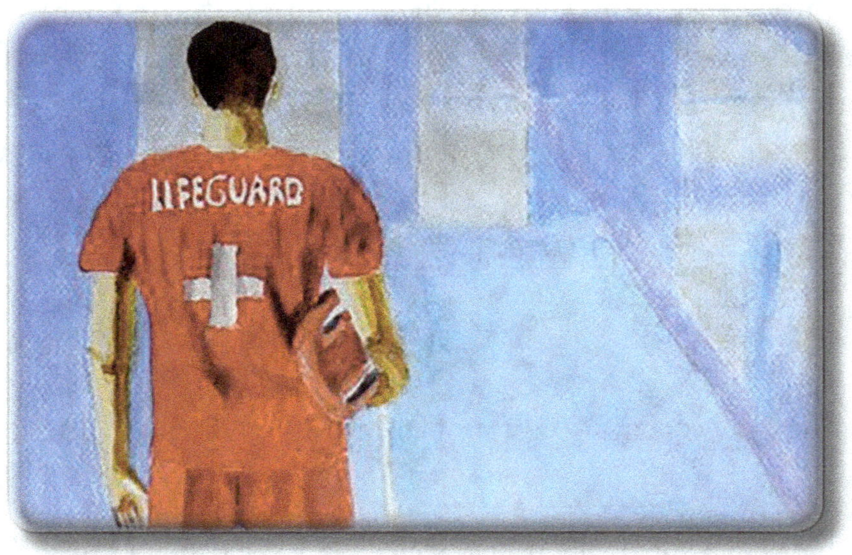

As the star breast stroke competitor on the Scarsdale swim team, Michael Bailey thought it would be fun to take a break before going to college and become a lifeguard. Consequently, he took the Red Cross certification program during spring break, which includes patron surveillance, rescue skills, victim assessment, first aid and CPR. Shortly after his certification, he got a job at the swimming pool of the Saint Andrew's townhouse complex of one hundred homes.

To be honest, it's not a particularly taxing job, especially in a small apartment complex. On any given summer day, there might be five or six residents in the small pool. True, weekends would be slightly more crowded. Perhaps there might be forty visitors, most of whom just slathered their body with Coppertone and sunned on the chaise lounges.

The most difficult part of the job is to resist the temptation to just read a book under the umbrella. Of course, that's verboten even with only a half- dozen people in pool. The young kids and their friends can be a challenge, but the major job of the lifeguard is to remind them that there should be no running on the concrete platforms around the pool and no diving. And of course, no roughhousing in the pool. It's sort of like being a school disciplinarian.

Of course, when you are needed, it's a very important job—perhaps even a lifesaving job. But in his first ten weeks overseeing the pool, Michael never had to jump into the water to rescue a swimmer. Today that changed. Three eight-year-old boys were playing tag in the shallow end when a young kid named Adam got entangled with the tagger and felt an accidental knee to his chest. He went under water for a few seconds and came up screaming "Help! Help!"

Michael immediately dove into the pool and put his arms around Adam's back. He told the kid to just relax and try to breathe. Within about eight seconds, he lifted Adam up and out of the shallow end and checked to make sure that he hadn't swallowed too much water. He checked his eyes to make sure they weren't blurry. Then he asked the kid to sit next to him by the side of the pool and just relax for a while. After about four minutes, Adam pleaded to rejoin his buddies. Michael, the lifeguard allowed the boy to go, but he did tell the trio, "No more tag."

The next rescue mission was nine months later, and this one was slightly more daunting. An eighty-year-old woman was climbing the ladder to get out of the deep end when she lost her footing and knocked her head against the side of the pool. Within ten seconds, Michael was by her side and lifted the alarmed woman out the water. He then did some first aid on a slight cut that she had on her forehead. He walked her to her chaise lounge and offered to bring her a glass or water or a soft drink. The appreciative woman hugged his arm and said, "You're good."

Maybe he was, but other than those two instances in two years, he was completely bored. He applied and was accepted at Boston College. When he met with the counselor there who perused his résumé, she suggested she could probably get him a job as a lifeguard in the school pool.

"No, thanks," Michael answered, and he quipped, "I've already saved enough lives. But do you have jobs in the cafeteria? That could keep me busy, and that's all I require."

18

The Last Days of Chuckles

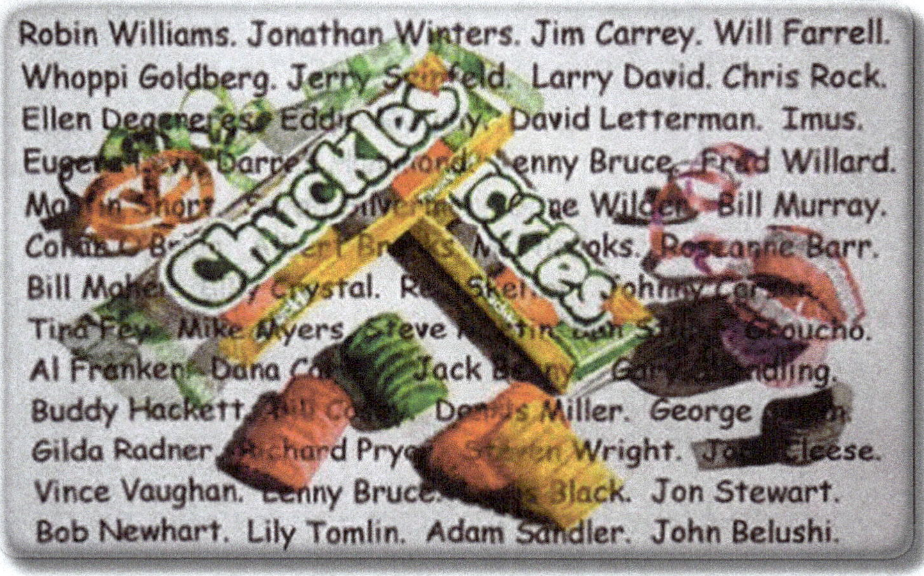

Charles "Chuckles" Carmichael passed away not so peacefully at his home in the Riverdale Section of the Bronx. He was ninety-six and had been in relatively good health for a man of his advanced age.

Chuckles spent the bulk of his career as a vaudeville comedian, and he often performed with Abbott and Costello in Manhattan, Los Angeles, Chicago, and dozens of other lesser-known cities such as Pittsburgh, Cleveland, and Topeka. In personality, he was often compared with Don Rickles for his rat- a-tat delivery and sarcastic humor.

He enjoyed a bountiful career well into his late sixties, when things changed for the entertainer. At the time, the type of comedy had evolved, and it was difficult for the veteran to find contemporary bookings. He tried tailoring his act to the more risqué times, but his jokes about getting laid and jerking off were considered out-of-step for a seventy-five-year-old man. Consequently, he called it quits twenty years ago and moved into an old folks' home—the Riverdale Senior Center—in the Bronx.

Despite the fact that he could not easily remember people's names (including his own son, whom he called "Whosit?"), he continued the jokes and gags until the very end. He enjoyed leaving those rubber dog poops in the hallways and those plastic vomit props in the coffee shop. He always got a giggle when he saw the staff come with their clean-up gear, only to realize that the displays on the floor were fake. "Hey, how funny is that?" he often exclaimed.

Just a few weeks ago, he told his son "Whosit?" that he hoped to one day die laughing. That happened this past Saturday. Mr. Carmichael was enjoying gummy bears and those jelly candies called Chuckles, when the attending nurse sat on a chair pillow in his room. Unbeknownst to her, there was a whoopee cushion under the pillow, which emitted a loud and long-lasting fart-like sound. The nurse screamed. Carmichael choked on one of the Chuckles while riotously laughing and expired within seconds.

Unlike most people, the former vaudevillian did get his dying wish.

May he rest in peace with a smile on his face.

19

Finally, a Birth

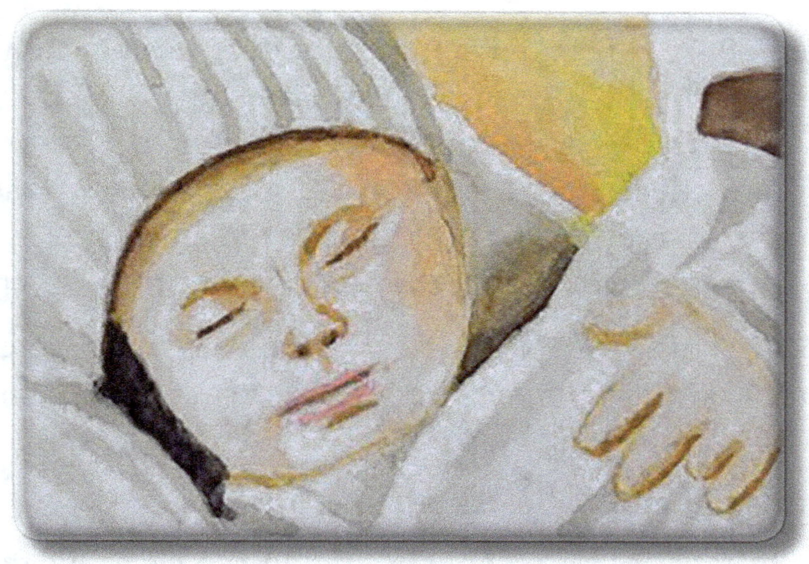

Maria Biasi had already suffered two miscarriages. They occurred in her early twenties when she was married to Aldo. According to her ob-gyn, they were isolated cases—one due to a bacterial infection, the other due to an immune disorder. In the wake of her tragedies, the doctor told her they were not necessarily connected, and quite possibly, she could bear a child in the years to come—if she was willing to try again.

For many years, she was not. After an ugly divorce from Aldo, and in her late twenties, Maria made her way as a single woman in Manhattan. She had a degree in business from Hunter College and was able to secure a choice position at Charles Schwab.

After six years of independent success at the firm, she began to feel lonely and reached out to Match.com. As a very attractive and financially secure woman in Manhattan, she gained many entreaties. At first, she was reticent to reply, but after tens of "interests" every week, she decided to give it a try.

To be perfectly honest, she was a reluctant catch. However, the flattery of the men she would meet was seductive. Sometimes she would have coffee with an interested party. Sometimes a glass of wine. Occasionally a dinner.

Even more occasionally, a night at her or his apartment.

She was reluctant for sexual encounters, especially in this day and age. It was difficult to ask if her date was tested for AIDS or sexually encountered diseases. Ugly! A real turn off. On the other hand, it's a matter of life and death. And yet, in the grips of supposed long-lost love, it was nice to feel appreciated and even embraced. As you may remember, one thing leads to another … and another … and another.

After three months of these new adventures, she began to feel stomach cramps and went back to her doctor, who advised her that she may be a pregnant.

"Are you kidding me?" she asked.

"Well, we should do more checks in the next few weeks," the doc advised.

Within the next few months, it was conclusive. Maria was indeed pregnant.

In view of her intermittent sexual encounters, it would be impossible to ascertain which Match.com paramour might have the sperm to make it happen. More importantly, Maria did not wish to know.

She also went to her ob-gyn every month to see if a miscarriage was in the offing. According to all medical indications, it was not.

And so she checked into Lenox Hill hospital without a husband or a boyfriend or even a stranger. Instead she asked her father to watch over her as she bore his first grandchild.

Miraculously, the baby was born without a single problem. Within minutes, Maria's father was in the delivery room and gushed. "I'm gonna name him Mario after you," the new mother told her father. "Want to hold him?"

"He's so tiny! Yes, but I don't want to drop him," he gushed. "Then just be very, very careful," Maria cautioned her dad.

In these days in the USA, you only get a day or two in the hospital. Then you are expected to leave. Maria did so with her father, who generously ordered a limo for their trip back to her Upper West Side apartment. He slept on the couch for two days to make sure his daughter and his new grandson were OK.

"I can't believe you are a momma." He hugged his daughter.

"I can't believe you are a grandpa," she answered, and she held up Mario for a kiss from his granddad.

"When do you have to go back to work?"

"Two or three months," she answered with a shrug. "But I will never be so aggressive in the day-to-day business."

"Maybe you'll be even better," Dad answered. "You may have a better sense of what is important to your customers—kids, family, grandpas, grandkids. It isn't all about capital gains."

"I've already realized that," Maria said, and she kissed her dad. After a pause and a long-lasting admiring look at his daughter, Mario answered. "If you ever need me here, I will be here. And I am very, very, very proud of you." He then kissed his grandson on the cheek and anxiously looked forward to a semi-needy call from his daughter. Actually, not even semi-needy. If Maria called him in the next few weeks and said that young Mario would like to see his grandfather, he would be there in a flash.

20

The Trayvon Effect

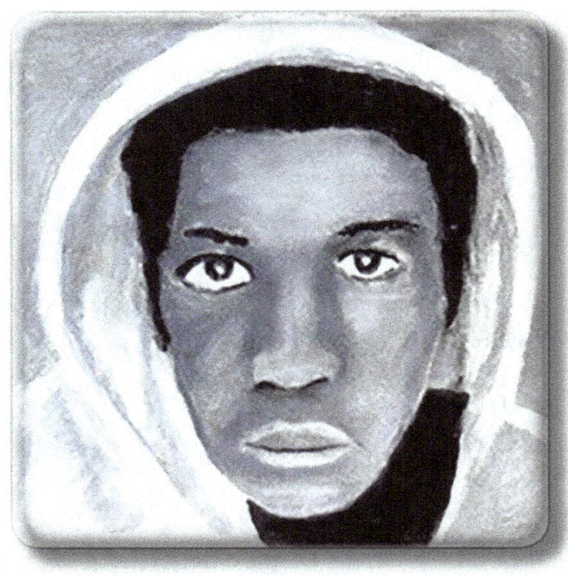

Trayvon Martin was not a perfect saint. He had been suspended twice in high school—once because the school found traces of marijuana in an empty envelope in his backpack (with no actual marijuana in the bag). His second offense? Jewelry was found in his backpack without a receipt. Note: no store or person had ever claimed any stolen jewelry that matched the earrings and necklaces. Even so, he was viewed as a troubled kid and was sent a message by his high school to get his act together. However, that is not a reason to shoot a teenage kid in cold blood, but that is apparently what happened on the evening of February 26, 2012.

On that late afternoon, he was walking through a 260-unit gated townhouse development in Sanford. Florida to visit his father several blocks away. As he strolled down the inner sidewalks, a neighborhood watch captain named George Zimmerman noticed "the intruder." He called the Sanford Police, reporting a "suspicious person." The cops immediately told him to stay put.

Exact words: "Do not approach the person. We will be there shortly."

He ignored that command. Instead, he evidently accosted the seventeen-year-old kid and engaged in a scuffle. According to a cell phone call to Trayvon's girlfriend, the young man claimed that someone was following him. She heard "Stop. Stop," from the young man. Moments later, neighbors reported gunfire. When officer Timothy Smith arrived shortly thereafter, George Zimmerman was discovered with blood oozing from his nose and the back of his head. On a more tragic note, young Trayvon Martin lay lifeless and bloodied on the inner sidewalk, with bullets in his body.

Not surprisingly, this created a national brouhaha. Jesse Jackson, Al Sharpton, Spike Lee, and the NAACP cried foul. They demanded justice on behalf of this innocent young black teenager who was gunned down by a white security guard.

By contrast, George Zimmerman claimed self-defense and was ultimately exonerated by the Florida courts since there was no other eyewitness who could refute his version of the story. Duh! The only other eyewitness was killed with George Zimmerman's bullets.

As sad as this tale is, it is not the end of the story. It has become a cautionary tale for every young black man in the country. Almost every African American parent now must warn their kids, "Be careful. It's a dangerous world for you out there."

In Ferguson, Missouri, the unarmed Michael Brown, at age eighteen, was shot and killed by a Ferguson police officer. The grand jury declined to charge the cop.

In Cleveland, Tamira Rice, at age twelve, was shot and killed by police for carrying a toy BB gun.

Similar things happened in Baltimore, Milwaukee, California, Phoenix, South Carolina, New York City, and hundreds of other locales. In fact, in the past few years, there have been 289 shootings of unarmed African American men and teenagers. As a matter of fact, young blacks are five times more likely to be killed by police than white folks. And still we wonder about race relations. Really?

BTW, as relates to the watershed Trayvon Martin incident, George Zimmerman expressed some concern that Trayvon may have been armed since he had his hand in one of his pockets. Hence, the self- defense plea.

Care to know what he had in his pocket and backpack? A bottle of watermelon fruit juice and a packet of Skittles.

I guess in some people's twisted imagination, that's worth bullets.

21

The Icky Obituary

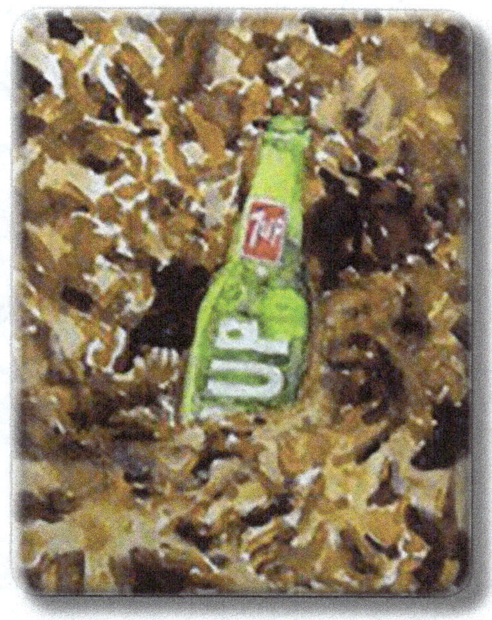

Bridget Wainright had already begun to feel that she was not cut out for this entry-level PR position. The assignment this weekend would further convince her.

She had taken the job at 7UP against her father's advice. "It's a cushy, damn office job for propaganda hacks," he argued. His criticism was not unexpected. Bob Wainright was the editorial chief of the *Saint Louis Post Dispatch* and considered any nonjournalistic writing a waste of time. "I can get you a real job on the staff with the snap of a finger," he promised.

That was exactly what the young Mizzou J-school grad didn't want—a daddy placement. Besides, 7UP offered some nice perks. Among them, she wouldn't have to rub shoulders with all those cursing, whiskey-drinking, cigarette-smoking reporter friends of her dad.

In her first few months at 7UP, she had written a puff piece about the recycling efforts in their Mankato bottling operation. She had created TV talking points for their brave new bottle design and submitted a story to Ad Age for their new groundbreaking media campaign.

Today she would be given a juicier assignment.

"What you write will undoubtedly appear in the Post," her boss, Ted Coniglio, told her. He then reached for his credenza and brought out a thick file. "We need an obituary for our former CEO, Dan Quinlan. Great man. All the details should be here—achievements, honors, speeches, family names."

Bridget looked over the documents to make sure she had all the information she would need. "It doesn't indicate when he died."

"Just leave that part blank," Coniglio answered, and he started to read his incoming telephone messages.

"Blank?"

"Well, he hasn't quite died yet. But it's imminent," her boss replied. "Icky," the woman involuntarily responded, somehow pulling out a

term from her grade school days. It embarrassed her to react so unprofessionally, but it did aptly describe how she felt.

"Icky or not, you can't really do these things after the fact. That's business.

We've got to stay ahead of the curve."

Over the weekend, Bridget struggled through several drafts. The past tense of the piece gave her fits—especially since Mr. Quinlan was still breathing.

On Monday, she presented several versions to Coniglio, who accepted them with minimal editorial revisions. "These are beautiful. Glorious, really! You've got a knack for this kind of writing."

On Tuesday, after a conversation with her father, she resigned from 7UP. In her first interview at the Post Dispatch, the city editor admitted that the entry-level job would include a lot of grunt work. "Council meetings mostly. But the politics are real, the emotions can be raw, and if you're lucky, there might even be some legit news. Just remember, the real story isn't always what's speechified in the meetings. A lot of that is just pure bullshit posturing. You gotta cut through that. How's it sound?"

"Cool," she answered. The word icky didn't even pop in her head.

Four weeks later, when reading the paper, she discovered the long article on the recently deceased Bob Quinlan. It was a glowing homage to the former CEO. They were all her words, and that made her feel wonderful for the man.

Sort of, but not really.

After folding up the paper, she went outside the building for a quick smoke.

Then she jauntily returned to her cubicle to cover the behind-the-scenes grit and intrigue of the latest city council meeting.

22

The Pen

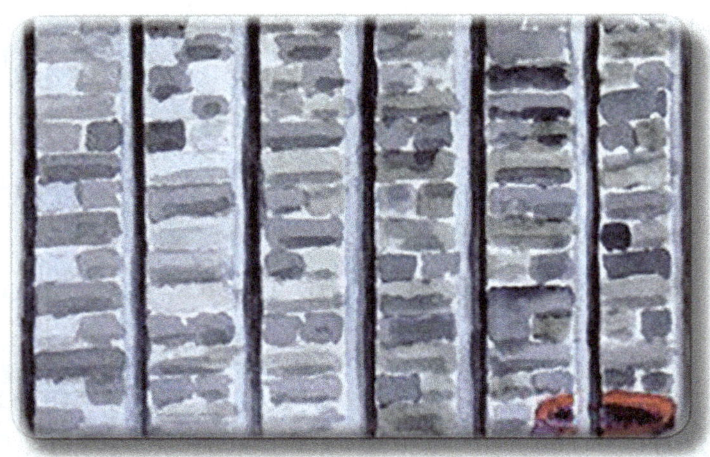

It felt bad being behind bars.

Like everyone in my situation, I felt I had done nothing to deserve this.

True, I had been homeless. But so were many others, and they continued to roam the street, live by their wits, and enjoy their freedom.

It was just an unlucky break that I was found in some guy's open garage when he returned in his fancy BMW. It's not like I was trying to steal his John Deer riding mower! I was just looking around, searching for a warm space, and the guy panicked on me. I thought I was going to have a heart attack. He called the authorities, and here I am—in the pen with way too many others.

Some of them are sick. Some are hostile. Most are, frankly, pretty nasty characters. I don't blame them. In most cases, they never got a break in life. That's just the way the dice roll, I guess. I'm not excusing it, but I'll tell you this: it isn't easy when others who are raised in the lap of luxury surround you.

It's raining outside right now, so I guess that's one upside to being incarcerated here. There are other compensations. The food is passable. It's served to us a couple of times a day. It's gruel, really. It's pushed inside the space of one big bowl. If you don't fight for your share, you are shafted. So you must dig in when it's dinnertime, hungry or not.

On many other levels, the conditions are deplorable. Some of the prisoners shit on the floor. The smell of urine is everywhere. When we do get visitors, the wardens hose down the place to make it presentable, but it's all an act for the visitors.

Oh, and one more thing I've noticed in my two-day incarceration: occasionally, the more cantankerous souls disappear. The guards identify the malcontents and lead them away. Those prisoners never return. I shudder to think what happens, but I try not to think of it. Especially not now. The place has been hosed down, and it's evidently visiting time.

Several families come in and stare at us. One mother and young son have stopped right in front of our cell. The kid seems to looking right at me. He's pointing. I realize I have an advantage over many others in that I am small, young, and have long hair.

"I like that one," the kid says.

"What kind of dog is it?" the mother asks.

"Mixed breed like most," the warden answers. "Probably part cocker, and part golden."

The warden opens the door and pulls me out by my collar. I am smart enough to behave myself in front of the kid. I rub my body against his leg and feel him pet me. It feels damn good.

"Can I name him Mookie?" the kid asks his mother.

I'm not crazy about the name, but it's no time to complain. So I nuzzle up to the young boy like the name is a natural.

"Mookie it is," the mom says, and she gives a thumbs-up to the warden.

Within fifteen minutes and tons of additional paperwork, I evidently have this new family. I look back at my old inmates and bark a goodbye. I hope I will never return. The kid hugs me and calls me Mookie again. I lick his face.

If I play my cards right, I think I may have just entered that lap of luxury which most of us have only dreamed of.

23

A Long Way Down

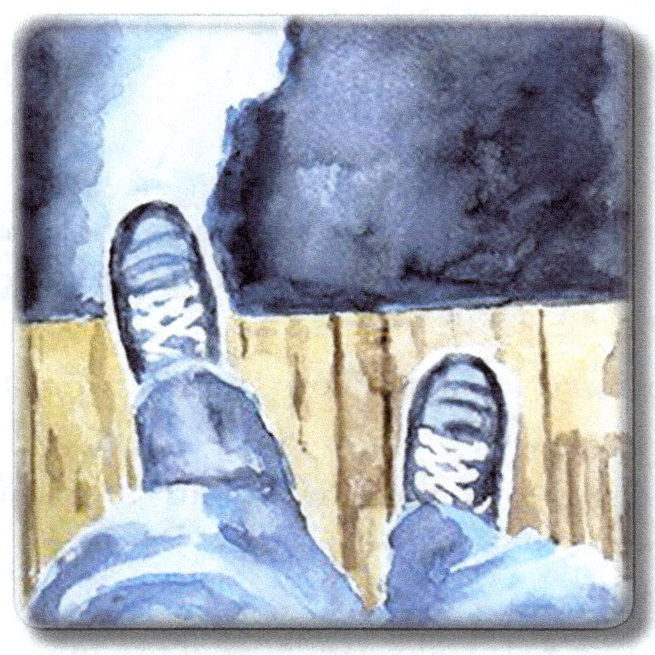

There are signs along the Tappan Zee Bridge that read *Life Is Worth Living.*

Presumably, they were placed there to discourage troubled souls from leaping into the waters of the Hudson River.

Perhaps Clarence Adderly had not observed the posted messages. More likely, he chose to ignore them.

I was following behind Mr. Adderly when his Chevy Malibu slowed to a stop in the right lane. "Damn, I can't believe it," I instantly reacted, frustrated that I would now be delayed on this rush hour traffic because of a stalled car.

When I saw him leave his Malibu and start climbing up to ledge, it became clear to me that the problem was not a disabled vehicle. It was a disabled human spirit.

"Don't jump!" I screamed out to the man as I raced from my blocked car.

Don't misunderstand; I am not a natural Good Samaritan, just a sixty-year old salesman trying to move through life. But I couldn't just sit there and watch a suicide in the making.

"Go away," Adderly called back to me as he held the heavy wire cable.

I took this as a good sign. Maybe the presence of an audience would be enough to discourage the act. As I inched forward, I prayed that some other driver would be calling 911. If only I could keep him from offing himself until the professionals arrive.

"Give me one reason not to jump," the man said, staring at the abyss.

A litany of rationales flooded my brain— "Because people love you," "Because tomorrow will be better," "Because it's selfish." None of them felt adequate.

"Can't think of one, can you?" Adderly taunted me.

"Because it will hurt," I said.

"I already hurt."

"Exactly, so this is not a good way to go," I countered.

For the next five or six minutes, we discussed alternative methods— a painless overdose, an instant gunshot, numbing carbon monoxide. By now the impatient New York drivers were blaring their horns, unwittingly egging him on. Where the hell are the trained psychologists? I thought.

We continued talking. For the next ten minutes or so, we discussed the pros and cons of each means, and the extra of pain of this particular style of suicide. It seemed to be sinking in.

"You think it's cold down there?" the man asked, peering over the ledge. "Icy and hard," I said. "And it's a long way down."

After an excruciating pause, Adderly heaved a huge frustrated, boozy sigh and eased himself down off the bridge. "You've given me some things to think about," the man told me, and he stumbled toward his car.

"Not so fast," I said as gently as I could. "You should really talk to someone."

"There's no one."

"There's me," I said, and I scribbled my home phone number on a business card. I gave it to Adderly, whose pores exuded that one-and-always familiar smell of liquor.

He never called. Hopefully, he awoke from his stupor the next morning, looked at himself in the mirror and got help. Given his pain, it's not inconceivable that he eventually took the easier route—the painkiller overdose. I never found out.

At least it didn't happen on my watch.

You can't save yourself unless you want to, I told myself. I looked at my unopened bottle of Smirnoff vodka across from my desk. Given the ordeal, I admit to being more tempted to take a sip than I had in the past seven years and four months of my sobriety. *One day at a time*, I reminded myself.

24

Good Guys vs Bad Guys

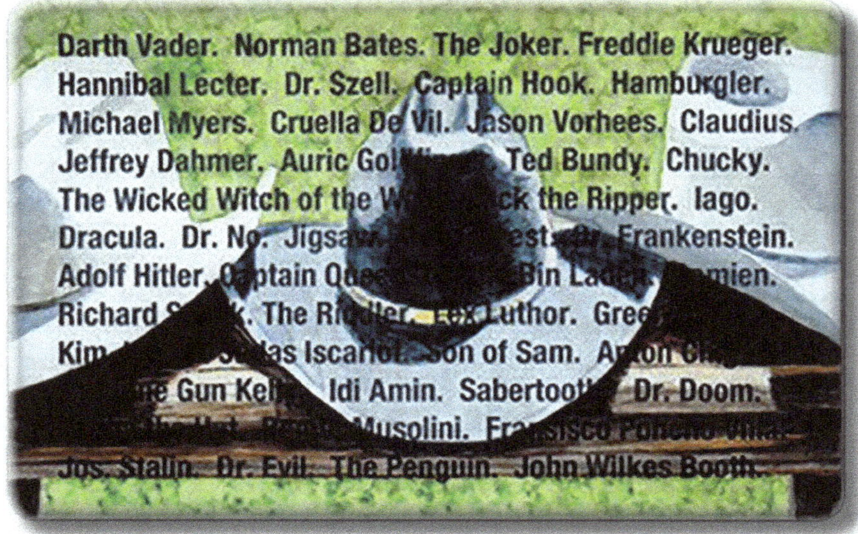

I was raised in a world of white cowboy hats and dark sheep. At this time, the good always prevailed over evil, at least in the movies. The gallant, courageous hero would always shoot out the villain and ultimately off him and ride into the sunset over the orchestral theme.

It doesn't always happen that way in real life. At least, it doesn't happen as easily as in movies.

Case in point: a recent incident in Cheyenne, Wyoming. It was a horse-riding adventure tour called "See the Real West." It included seven tourists and a tour guide through the glorious mountains and streams of this naturally wonderful area.

All the participants seemed to be impressed with the panoramas. Well, almost all. There was one aggressive soul who would repeatedly ask, "Where are the cowboys? Where are the villains? Show us where the gunfights happened out here."

Most of the others would ask about the geography or the nature of the horses. A young woman named Ellen became frightened as her horse began to canter down the hill. "Whoah, whoah, whoah," she called out to her steed, and she tried to pull back on the reigns.

The belligerent loudmouth behind her was quick with criticism. "Can't you control your damn horse?" he yelled.

The guide, a twentysomething guy called Brad helped grab the stirrups of Ellen's horse and returned her and her brown quarter horse to the pack.

"Amateur! Amateur!" Victor, the villain, scoffed.

At this point, the tour guide raised his hand as a preset rehearsed signal to the group that everyone should stop and listen. "OK, let me reset the ground rules once again. We're all out here as a group and to have some fun. So no one is allowed to criticize others. Do you understand?" He looked at the ugly personality in the black cowboy hat. "I think it's going to work out best if you trail the pack and look out for your compadres in front of you."

"I don't like to be bossed around," Victor snarled.

"I don't like malcontents," Brad, the tour guide, answered.

"Wow, Mr. Big Word! What? Did you go to college just to get a dumb shit job riding horses up a mountain?"

Silently, Brad took the lead of the group, and they walked horses up the steep incline of the mountain. While they did so, the tour leader took out his cell phone and called the camp to report that he was having some trouble with the group.

"Glad you called," the woman at the home base said. "There are a couple of cop cars waiting here. Evidently, there is one guy in the group who is an escaped convict and a real hothead. According to the cops, he could be armed and dangerous."

"I know exactly who he is," Brad responded, and he looked back at the group behind him. When he looked back toward the last guy, he saw the man still in line but giving him the finger. The next thing Brad knew, he heard galloping hooves. When he looked around, he saw the villain gaining ground on the group and pulling out a pistol. He had it aimed at Brad. "Take this, asshole!" the bad guy screamed and aimed his gun at the tour leader.

Brad, of course, knew how to handle a horse better than 99 percent of the population. He steered his horse aggressively and suddenly to the left and dodged the bullet. Fearful for the safety of his group, he pulled out his holstered six-shooter and aimed at the mad horseman who was racing up the incline to his right.

Pow! One sure shot, and the villain fell off his horse, like they were in an ugly moment in a cowboy movie.

The tour guide held up his hand, signaling that everyone should just sit tight on their horses. He then approached the man who had been shot out of his saddle. As he did so, he saw the ugly, pained man writhing in pain. He was also reaching for his gun in retaliation. Before he could reach the pistol, Brad delivered two more bullets into his chest, and the man ceased to breathe. He then gathered the villain's horse and brought the innocent creature back to the front of the pack. When he returned, he addressed the very frightened group of six.

"It's all over," Brad said. "Don't be afraid. Don't be worried. We are only about a half mile from the camp, and we will go slowly, carefully and very, very safely the rest of way."

When they reached the camp, most of tourists on horses cried and hugged. At this gathering point, there were now four police cars with rotating red lights.

The cops immediately approached the tour guide. They explained that the dangerous man had escaped from prison and told his friends that he hoped to escape into the mountains on horseback.

"Where is he? What happened?" the chief of police asked.

Brad explained the gunfight in the mountains of Cheyenne, and that the man was now dead half a mile off the northern trail.

Not surprisingly, the police officers asked all the people on the tour to help with an eyewitness account of events. As each one did, they broke down in tears, praised Brad for his heroism, and then hugged him for securing their safety.

After six interviews, the cops asked where the remains of the bad guy could be.

"Up that a way," Brad responded like a hero cowboy. "Do I need to go up there?"

"Not really. If we can't find the bad guy, we will call you. We have your number." Then the police chief reached out his hand to congratulate the hero.

"I just want to say thanks. Today, you saved six people's lives and eliminated a vermin that would inevitably be in court cases for the next seven to eight years. Instant justice," the chief summed it up.

The other ten police officers came up to Brad, and each, in a simpatico move, shook hands with him or hugged him.

Given the fact that there are very few modern westerns, Brad occasionally searches for them on cable. Very occasionally, he finds one. When he does, he easily identifies with the good guy.

Seeking Human Kindness

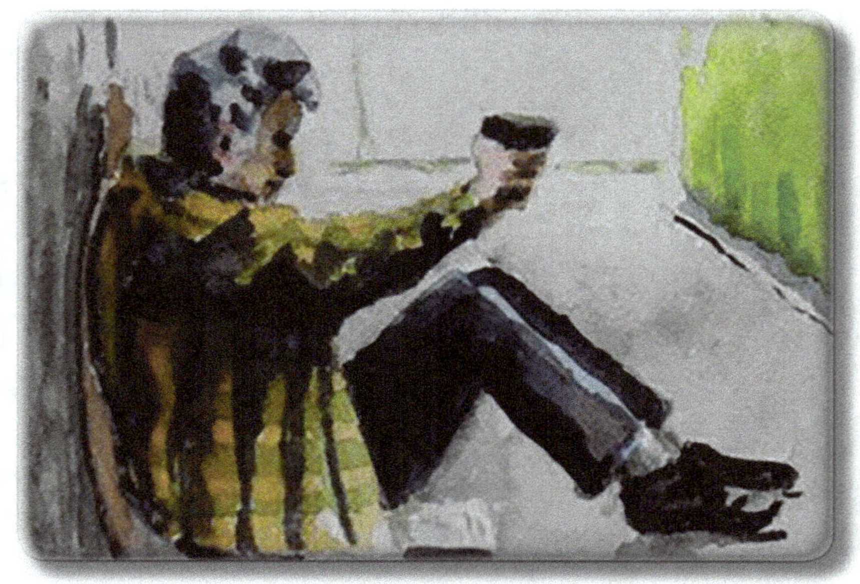

On most days when I walked to the subway, I saw the man wrapped in a blanket on Thirtieth and Third Avenue. He was always scruffy, tired, and sad, especially on the chillier mornings. I judged him to be about sixty, but in these circumstances, one never knows. With a difficult life, he might have been decades younger and just prematurely wrinkled.

Normally, the guy had a handwritten sign perched by his feet that said Homeless and Hungry. Sometimes, when that cardboard would get too flimsy or too wet, he would vary the wording to Need Help or God Bless You.

Often I would reach in my pocket and give the beggar a quarter or two.

Sometimes if I was short of change, I would chip in a dollar. Other than that, I didn't think of the vagrant much. Until last night.

I was on a date with a woman I had met last week at Gramercy Tavern. Her name was Joanie, and she was a real beauty with a nice sense of humor. We laughed almost all night together, even in bed. I admired the fact that she called me the next afternoon and asked for a repeat performance. What spunk! I also admired her ambition and lifestyle. A recent graduate of Columbia, she already had a sweet job at Chase Manhattan.

By contrast, I was an urban planner with a desire to help create a New York that wasn't just overrun by millionaires. I helped the city plan for apartment buildings that would at least open up some floors for the middle class and the less fortunate among us. It didn't pay as handsomely as my MBA buddies' cushy jobs, but my bigger compensation was that I always believed the job was important.

Joanie and my disparity in career paths didn't seem to alter our attraction to each other. Perhaps it was just the sexual urge. It could also be the tenor of the times. We both had enough to cover our individual rents, and in this day and age, men and women often split the dinner and entertainment bills, so it's not an all-male financial burden. Thank God for progress.

After some passionate kissing in my apartment, Joanie and I almost cancelled our dinner reservation, but we ultimately decided we could regain our momentum after dinner.

As we walked toward my favorite neighborhood restaurant, Artisanal, I fantasized about the cheese fondue, the crème brûlèe, and several hand- wrapped packages from their fromagerie. OK, I admit it —I also fantasized about the almost inevitable late-night fun and hugs under the blankets.

Speaking of blankets, I saw that familiar homeless man under his torn and soiled blanket as Joanie and I walked hand in hand toward Thirty-Fourth Street.

I looked at him. As usual, he had his head low with a cup and a sign in front of him. He looked up at me and waved wearily.

"Wow, you got a new sign," I volunteered. It read Seeking Human Kindness. "I like it." I then reached in my pocket, but I could find no change.

In fact, I didn't have anything smaller than a twenty-dollar bill. I immediately turned to my date. "Joanie, do you have any spare change. Or maybe a dollar?"

"Josh!" she scolded me through clenched teach. "Don't help the worthless."

I admit to being stunned by her comment, and I simply told the homeless man that I didn't have any spare change but would most likely have it on my way home after dinner.

"I really just need food," he responded. "If you can give me your scraps, I can probably survive for a few more days."

"Count on it," I told him, and I walked with Joanie toward my fancy-shmantzy eatery. This time, however, we did not walk hand in hand.

Once inside the place, we ordered. Inevitably, we did get into a discussion about our very different values.

She opened up the debate. "It's ignorant to think that that man couldn't get a real job. He probably wants money just for drugs. Come on. This is the land of opportunity. Anyone who wants to succeed can succeed."

My riposte: From my job as an urban planner, I knew otherwise. In point of fact, America has a 13.5 percent poverty rate. Translation: 93 million people in the great USA live in poverty. More to the point, 560,000 individuals in this great country of ours are homeless.

"Do you think he was once successful? Do you think he had a wife? Do you think his kids know him? Do you think he knows what's happening to him?

"He's a loser. He's hopeless. He has no redemptive qualities."

This back-and-forth debate went on for the next thirty minutes, after which we decided to nix dessert and call it a night. On the Park Avenue side of the restaurant, I hailed a cab for Joanie and gave her an obligatory hug.

On my way home from the restaurant, I dropped off a few packages of artisanal cheese for my lonely homeless man. One was Emmentaler. The other was a brie. Just for good measure, I also brought him some biscuits and plastic knives.

I regret to inform you that it was the last time I saw the man on

Thirtieth and Third. Admittedly, I did have to go out of town for a few days after that event. *Maybe he moved to a new location*, I tried to reassure myself. Maybe he moved to a shelter, I wondered.

Of course not, I told myself.

I kept looking at his homeless spot for the next seven days. He was no longer there. There was a torn blanket at his place, but no human being.

I never saw him again.

Just to complete the circle, I never saw Joanie again either.

26

Christmas in August

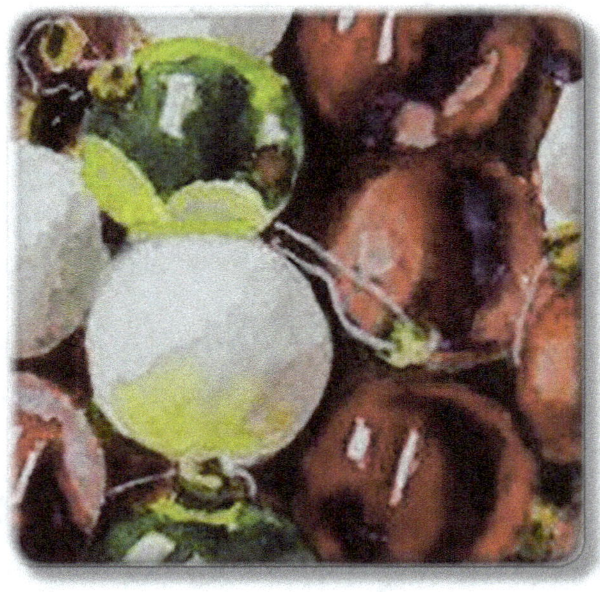

At the risk of being an oracle of the obvious, no young kid should ever get cancer and struggle with survival. However, such things do happen and sometimes (not always) end with a relatively positive ending.

For the past four years, Barry Cooper has struggled with leukemia. The young man was diagnosed at age three after losing much weight and feeling weak almost every hour of the day.

His worried parents had taken him to their family doctor in Ohio, who suggested a battery of tests—MRIs, CAT scans, and of course, blood tests.

After two months of such procedures, their doctor suggested that it could be cancer and that the young lad go to a specialist.

"Cancer?" his mother sobbed.

"Could be. It happens. I think he should see a specialist in the field. As you know, the earlier you catch it, the better his chance of survival," the doctor said,

"Survival?" the dad responded in shock.

"Let's take this one step at a time." The doctor tried to calm the

alarmed parents. With his recommendation, the parents were able to enroll young Barry in the Cincinnati Children's Hospital, which is ranked near the top for all pediatric cancers.

It has been a harrowing past three years. Barry has had lots of chemotherapy to try to arrest the growth of this bone marrow cancer that tends to afflict the young. Consequently, he has lost most of young childhood.

As Dr. Kingham at the children's hospital said, "The odds will increase in his favor the longer he can last. In fact, the odds have increased every decade since 1990."

No parent likes to hear that his dear son's life is a matter of odds.

"So what's the survival rate as of today?" Dad asked.

"It's above eighty percent," the doctor bragged.

"So twenty percent are buried," the dad soberly assessed.

"Yes," Dr. Kingham answered, knowing that honesty is a wiser course of action than rah-rah-rah cheerleading. "But as we have discussed in earlier meetings, your son is already at stage four."

The next day Mr. and Mrs. Cooper applied to Saint Jude's Children's hospital in Memphis, Tennessee, on behalf of their ailing son, Barry. The parents had heard that this nurturing institution was the best in the country for pediatric cancer research. Also they believed that a new set of eyes and diagnoses could give them more hope.

Young Barry was not so thrilled about relocating to a part of the country he barely knew. "I just want to be with my friends," the young boy said.

"Besides, I want to be with both of you."

"We will be down there every weekend," his mother reassured her son. "Besides, you will be in a living condition with other young boys and girls who are trying to get better just like you. It might be fun!"

It was the first time Mrs. Copper had used the word *fun* in years.

It was not fun. For the parents, the weekend commute was a nightmare.

However, young Barry did seem to be quite content with the treatment and caring environment at Saint Jude's.

Every week, they would have a consultation with his primary physician, who always had a thick file of test results and combined medical opinions from the staff.

After seven months, the doctor had a "come to Jesus" meeting with Mr. and Mrs. Cooper.

"We have run three dozens of test, but our diagnosis is that it is terminal cancer," he said.

"How long?" his dad soberly asked. "Two months."

"Does Barry know?"

"Not specifically. But being here, every kid does get the idea that it might not be forever."

"When should we take Barry home?" his sobbing mother asked. "Anytime that's convenient for you."

On the eight-hour drive back to Cincinnati, the family mostly listened to music and privately pondered the days ahead. Eventually, brave young Barry raised the topic, "What did the doctors at Saint Jude say?"

"It's not so good," his dad answered.

"I know it's not so good. I am eight years old and have a bald head, and I'm in pain. So what's the verdict?"

"We'll talk about it when we get home … in about twenty minutes." "I want to know," Barry asserted.

Within twenty-five minutes, they were in their home and dear Dad answered his son's question.

"It's terminal," Dad answered. "Do you know what that means?"

"Duh, I have been in cancer hospitals for the past four years. Of course, I know."

"Two or three months," Mom cried. "End of summer," Barry calculated.

"Yep," Dad gulped.

"Shucks, I'd hate to miss Christmas." Barry slumped and hugged Mom and Dad for many minutes.

"'I'd hate to miss Christmas,'" Mrs. Angela Cooper repeated to her neighbor the next day over a long cup of coffee.

"So he won't," Bernice, the neighbor, told her. "We'll organize Christmas in August. We'll make it a surprise! A Christmas tree by the pool, and presents for everyone. All the neighborhood kids will love it. And so will Barry! And if he miraculously pulls through, it'll mean two Christmases."

"I don't think that's in the cards," Angela pulled out a Kleenex and wiped away a tear.

"So it will be the most unusual, most memorable Christmas ever," Bernice answered, and she hugged her friend.

By the end of July, she had notified twenty neighbors to bring a gift for Barry and at least one for their own kids. She found a pine tree in the local nursery and retrieved her bundles of Christmas lights and ornaments. On the evening before the ceremony, she put up the tree and strung the lights.

By seven o'clock the next evening, Mr. and Mrs. Cooper and young Barry arrived at their house.

"Wow, what's with all the cars?" the young boy asked. "Who knows?" Dad answered.

When they walked through the fence to their backyard, they heard thirty- three neighbors begin singing, "We wish you a Merry Christmas."

Ironically, the little bald-headed boy broke down with emotions. Somehow, he had learned to steel himself for the inevitable, if only for the sake of his dear mom and dad, who he knew felt such pain. One by one, he opened his gifts by the lit tree near the outdoor pool and thanked everyone who had made this possible.

"This is the best Christmas ever," he told everyone over an open mike.

It truly was. Ever and ever. And it always will be for young Barry Cooper and for all those generous souls who attended the Yuletide celebration in the backyard of the Coopers.

27

The New Capo

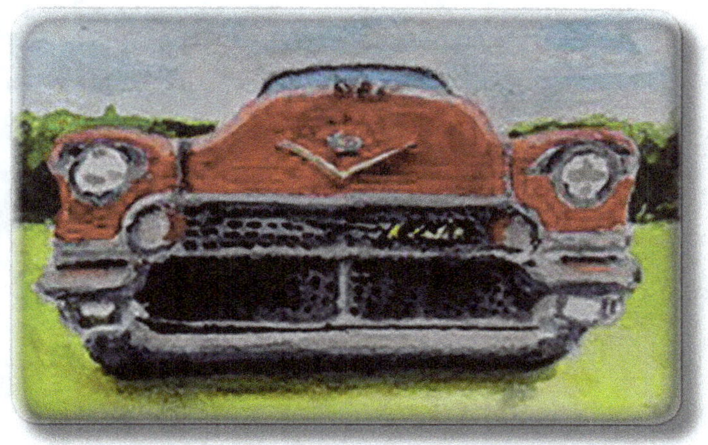

Mario Margherio always loved walking down Arthur Avenue in the Bronx.

For one thing, it was a haven of Italian restaurants and bakeries. More importantly, it felt like home for the Mafia don.

On any given day, he would park in the lot near Madonia Bakery, and give the attendant a very generous five-dollar bill just to keep his convertible safe.

At least once a week, he would ask the guy to wash his car and make it squeaky-clean. Normally, after such a procedure the attendant would put it in the prime parking spot to remind locals that the boss was in town.

After such a privileged parking experience, Mario would then walk into Ann & Tony's, Greco's, Emilia's, or any of a dozen other restaurants and enjoy a hug from the proprietor—along with a bulging white envelope, which the capo would promptly put in his suit pocket.

"What's fresh today?" Mario asked Luigi, the proprietor of Borgatta's, an establishment that had been going strong from eight decades.

"Ravioli in a red sauce," Luigi answered. "I'll make sure it comes

with fresh basil and parmesan for you."

Halfway through the meal, Luigi stood by the table, obviously looking for a compliment.

"It's *delicioso*," Mario volunteered. "And how are things? Any troubles in the neighborhood? Any difficulties with deliveries? Any inconveniences whatsoever?"

Luigi shrugged and shook his head no.

"If so, you gotta let me know." Mario gave his familiar speech. "I want you and your employees to feel safe and secure. You can't always count on the cops for that. But you can count on me."

"No problema," Luigi answered.

After handshakes all around, Mario then walked to Madonia Bakery to get fresh fennel bread and retrieve his cleaned convertible in the parking lot.

What a wonderful daily experience!

On the next day, Mario visited Domicks's restaurant. When he walked into the shop, it was the same familiar ritual—a hug, a stuffed envelope, and excellent lunch.

On this particular day, Giovanni (the owner) approached him at the capo's private table and asked a difficult question. "Do you know that Nikko from Little Italy is sniffing around the neighborhood to ascertain if they would like extra special protection?"

"You've got to be fucking kidding me," Mario answered. "Sotto voce," Giovanni responded. "But trust me, it's going on."

After a slice of tiramisu, Mario went back to his parking lot, caught the keys from this attendant, and drove off to his home just eight blocks away.

He was aware of the rivalry, but it had always been peaceful—as long as Little Italy thrived. But lately that Manhattan neighborhood had become less vital as Chinatown began to intrude on its territory.

In his heart, he knew there was no other territory other than this most historic Italianate section of the Bronx.

On the next day, he went back to Arthur Avenue and began his

reconnaissance. At Café al Mercado, he discovered that the same entreaties had occurred from Little Italy. At Randazzo's, he learned that the Nikko of Little Italy had actually tried to bring in a ledger sheet of services he could provide versus Mario.

"That's dishonorable," Mario protested, using the worst possible criticism in the Mafia.

The next noon, he went to Umberto's—the Arthur Avenue equivalent of the Little Italy spot where John Gotti was shot to death. When Mario walked out of the famous restaurant, he was assailed with a volley of bullets, which resulted in a slump on the sidewalk and then a surrender to the inevitable ending.

Despite the fact that it happened on a busy Saturday afternoon at 2:00 p.m., there were no apparent witnesses to this ugly slaughter, according to the police. Evidently, it was a rare moment when everyone was busy shopping in the meat markets, bakeries, or restaurants.

That late afternoon, Mario's prized convertible remained unclaimed in the parking lot across the street from Madonia Bakery. The attendant had washed the car that afternoon and made it spick-and-span. On Sunday he found Mario's address from some restaurateurs and drove the car back to its final resting place.

On the next Monday there was a religious service at Our Lady of Mount Carmel Church on Arthur Avenue. It was filled with hundreds of family members, friends, and business folks who wanted to pay tribute. Nikko from Little Italy also attended and paid his respects.

On the very next day, he visited the restaurants on Arthur Avenue, expressed his regrets, and began to build bonds with all the establishments along the street.

28

The Stairwell to Hell

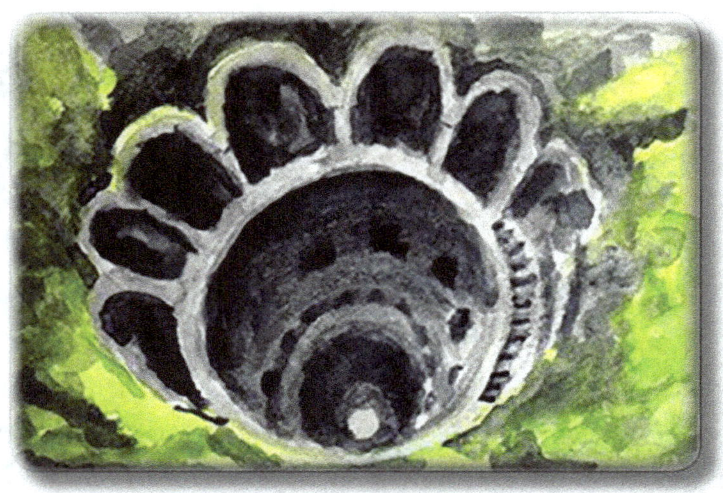

It's just weird.

I have been fortunate enough to see many of the world's most amazing man-made architectural achievements. Machu Picchu in Peru is absolutely stunning (and quite scary to climb). The Great Wall of China is positively breathtaking. The Red Square, la Tour Eiffel, even the Empire State Building are forever inspiring.

And then I went to Portugal—the new or ancient hot place to visit in Europe. Here, the architecture, the friendliness, the hills, and the style of this historic city are seductive. In many ways, it's an amazing place. And then I went to Sintra, which sits atop a many-mile mountain with centuries-old palaces and the most western-bound seashores.

After a morning of climbing up cobblestones in a castle called Quinta de Regaleira, one finds a place called the Initiation Well. It is based on *Dante's Inferno*, and symbolizes our descent into hell, heaven, or purgatory, depending on our decisions along the way. It's a small dark shaft guarded by two stone demons or dragons, with 163 downward very narrow circular steps that, if we choose right, leads us to a small pool of water—and presumably, safety.

It is not well lit. As a matter of fact, one must hold one's breath as you descend down the twelve-inch-high stairs. All along the way, you can look over the edge and see the daunting dark water. Ironically, that's the goal—to reach hell.

About halfway down, the tour guide calls out to the tourists. We have reached a crossroads. "Should we go right or go left?"

Most of my compadres agree to go right, especially in view of the fact that there is some light at the end of that tunnel.

"Nope, you all guessed wrong. We go left," the tour guide smugly answered.

After another four dark stairways, our tour guide asked the same questions.

Instinctively, we all pointed to the right since it once again exuded a faint light.

"Wrong again," he said. I began to realize that this was a game—admittedly a rather macabre game, but an exciting exploration all the same. And so we followed blindly until we reached the end, which indeed elicit a very faint light.

As I reached the end of my circular tunnel, I looked up again and saw the dark rounded stairwells of this mysterious attraction. I was relieved to have landed safely. Quite honestly, I wondered how many unescorted people had lost their lives stumbling down this treacherous stairwell. Three or more lost souls? A dozen? A hundred?

Just when we reached heaven's pond, we discovered another daunting challenge. As opposed to secure walkway, there were fifteen large rocks set in the water with the invitation to walk across to safety.

I'm in pretty good shape. I bike. I play tennis. But I don't always walk across slippery rocks that are at least fifteen inches from each other. One after another, my new friends slowly and cautiously walked across. My turn. I made it across the first ten blocks of rock and then paused. Not a good idea.

But after a deep breath, I was able to get across the pond.

Behind me was an eighty-year-old woman who was coaxed hand in hand by her husband up front and perhaps her son behind. After eight steps, she lost her balance (as did her family members). She fell into three feet of water, as did her family members.

Immediately, the tour guide jumped in the pond and rescued her. Obviously, the camera around her neck was destroyed. However, the tour guide did have a cell phone and snapped a memorial picture of the water-drenched woman, her husband, and her son.

I watched in wonder. "This could never happen in the USA," I told my buddy. "Not enough handrails. Not enough lighting. Too much danger. Too many deaths over the years."

"Too exciting," he responded.

In a weird, memorable way, I had to agree.

29

Zero Tolerance

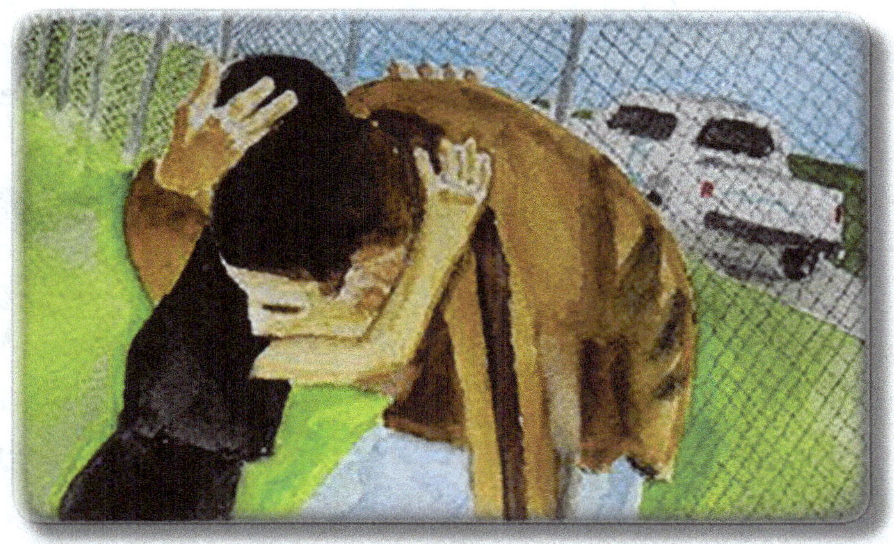

For most Americans, it's difficult to imagine raising your young son in an environment of gang violence and ruined economies. Despite the risks of leaving Las Nueces, Guatemala, and joining the caravan to the US border for almost 2,200 miles, Luis Cruz decided it was worth it on behalf of his ten- year-old son, Ervin.

Perhaps the deciding factor was when Ervin, a rather bright third grader, suddenly quit school to work in the coffee fields.

"Why?" his dad incredulously asked.

"I didn't have a choice," the kid explained. "One of the thugs in town told me I had to work for him or great harm would come to me or my family."

That night, Luis cried with his wife and decided that the best chance his son had was in the US, away from the crushing poverty of Guatemala. As he said, "When you've got a gun to your head and people threatening to rape your daughter, extort your business, and force your son to work for cartels, what would you do?"

"Ask for asylum," she agreed.

Given the attitude of the current administration, both parents agreed and understood that they would not be automatically accepted. But it was worth the chance. And if it worked, his wife and daughter could attempt the same journey next year after he was able to save some money, hopefully with work in the USA.

When they reached the Texas border in May, it was mayhem. Swarms of Guatemalans with their kids were housed in tents or in worse conditions.

Attorney General Jeff Sessions had just announced that people caught illegally crossing would face criminal prosecution and that the children would be separated. At least 1,995 kids were separated from 1,940 adults from April 19 to May 31, according to numbers released by the Department of Homeland Security.

The images of migrant children being separated from their parents raised an uproar in the US and around the world. As the time, he told the US guard, "If they separate us, they separate us. But return to Guatemala? That is something my son cannot do."

Fortunately, the dad was able to reach his grandparents, who were legal and worked on a farm in Louisiana. Given that fact, young Ervin was classified as an unaccompanied minor if his grandparents assumed custody. They drove down the next day to sign the papers and retrieve him.

That evening, Luis had his last hug with his son in the US. He told him that he was going to be able to go to school again, living with his grandparents.

Then he fibbed about the fact that when he went to school, Dad would have to work in Texas.

Instead of course, he was deported the next day. Deep down, Luis knew that he could probably raise a ruckus about his son's separation, but of course, that would most likely result in the young boy's deportation as well. No, this was a greater act of love. Being in the US was the kid's only chance of a decent life.

Ervin calls back to Las Nueces at least twice a week to speak with his dad or his mom. It's clear from every phone call that he misses them, but he does not miss the dangers and threats of Guatemala. According to Grandma, the kid is doing well in school.

"Maybe we can see each other next year," the young son said hopefully.

"That would be nice, but some things would have to change at the border,"

Dad admitted. "I'll keep my fingers crossed that it will happen someday." As was true with the conclusion of every call, Luis was conflicted about being separated from Ervin. But ultimately, he hoped his dear son would someday understand that it was all done out of love.

30

Shooting the Squirrel

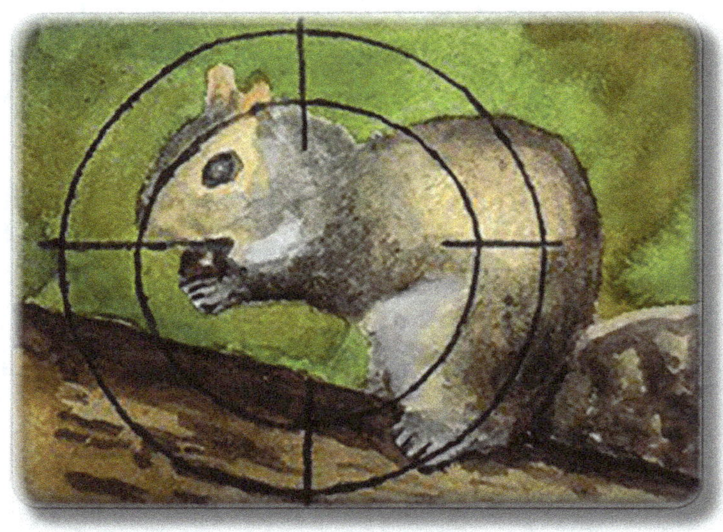

Zach Krouse was only nine years old and had never fired a gun in his young life. But on the family trip to his uncle's place in Herrin, Illinois, that was about to change.

It was only a few hours' drive from his Saint Louis home, but the Krouse family rarely visited Uncle Ed. His mom and her brother were after all very different siblings. She had gone to SIU, majored in English, moved to the big city, and then married and raised a family in the Saint Louis suburbs. Uncle Ed had stayed on the farm and occasionally worked in construction.

To be honest, Zack didn't really want to visit the rural sticks. "What will I do there?" he asked his mom.

"It's just a good thing to know your relatives," Mrs. Krouse told him.

After a few hours of reminisced childhood stories, Uncle Ed said, "Have you taught the boy how to shoot?"

"We don't have guns in the house," Mr. Krouse answered, trying not to sound too judgmental in front of his brother-in-law.

"Well, it's high time to learn some country ways." The uncle chuckled and looked over to young Zach. The boy looked at his mom and dad, who looked at each other.

"You be real careful, and follow the instructions of your uncle," his mom said.

"And, Ed, safety first," his dad warned.

"It's BBs," Ed reassured them. "But, of course, safety first. You know it."

Indeed, Ed did stress safety. He taught the boy how to walk with the rifle, how to point, how to focus. The uncle then put a dozen empty Pabst cans on the fence about twenty yards away. "Let's see how well you can aim."

Zach fired the rifle and missed the first four beer cans. His uncle gave him a few pointers, and the boys subsequently hit four of the next eight. "Wow, you're a natural marksman," Uncle Ed complimented him. "Let's see how well you do with a moving target."

"What do you mean?"

"An animal," Ed answered, and he started walking toward the woods.

"I don't want to shoot an animal," Zach said, following behind with his BB gun in the proper point-down position.

"Well, it ain't gonna be a real animal," Uncle Ed reassured him. "Just a squirrel or two. Varmint, really."

Zach didn't really like the idea. On some level, he could maybe understand some ancient pioneer shooting a deer or a moose for some winter food. He'd read about that in early American history. But this was not then, and this was not that.

"Shh, look," Uncle Ed whispered to the boy. He pointed to a squirrel on a tree trunk about forty yards away. "Take aim."

The boy reluctantly did so. It's just a squirrel, he said to himself. But the thought was instantly followed by the fact that the innocent rodent had never done anything to him. *Why did he deserve to die for target*

Zach took careful aim and saw the squirrel in his scope. Just before he squeezed the trigger, he pulled the weapon slightly right of the target.

"Missed," the boy said with real relief. "I've had enough."

At dinner, Ed boasted about the boy's progress. "Great kid. I really enjoyed that. When are you folks coming back to visit Uncle Ed?"

"Realistically, the school year is jammed. Maybe next summer," Mrs. Krouse answered.

"By then young Zack might be ready for a shotgun," the uncle said.

By then, the boy hoped he might have a full summer baseball schedule that would conflict with any further animal targets.

31

Halloween and the Day of the Dead

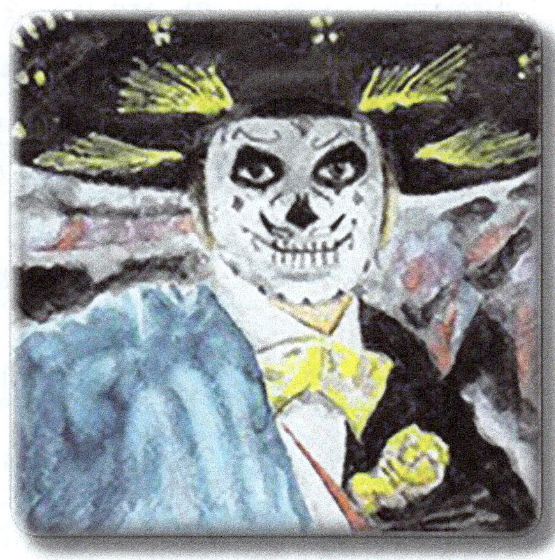

Ever since he was a preteen, Luis Rodriguez loved the holiday of Halloween.

For one thing, there was all that candy, and some of the larger homes in the Central West End of Saint Louis gave out those expensive bars like fifty-cent Nestlé Crunches, and larger bags of M&M's. Some even gave money.

Occasionally, there were dollars thrown in the Halloween bags. On those private gated streets, they evidently didn't have that many kid visitors, so they compensated with bigger treats in the hopes that it might prevent mischief.

Actually, that was the original appeal of this holiday for young Luis. As an altar boy raised in the Catholic faith, he knew that this strange holiday had some dark underpinnings. Liturgically, its formal name is All Hallows' Night, in commemoration of All Saints' Day the following morning and All Souls' Day (the good, the bad, and the ugly creatures of this world) the very next day. In that respect, it has always had ghoulish associations.

Also, as descendant of Mexican heritage, he had been taught about the Day of the Dead. As his grandfather, Papa Pedro, often explained to him that this holiday was about commemorating our loved ones who had passed away.

How to do that? With a wild festive celebration through the streets.

So in that respect, Halloween and the Day of the Dead intersected.

Most of all, Luis and his buddies loved the fact that the holiday was the only one where naughtiness was the order of the day. The TV commercials telegraphed the scary aspects of the howling moon. Modern movies simply underscored the point with films that lead to nightmares.

On Christmas, everyone must be angelic and filled with sweetness and light.

On the Fourth of July, we are all expected to be patriotic and watch a parade. On Easter Sunday, we're supposed to get all dressed up and attend a church service. But on Halloween, all bets are off. In his early teen days, Eddie and his buddies used to create some mischief in the neighborhood.

Their favorite practice was to TP a house. It's a fairly harmless inconvenience for the vacant homeowner who has refused to leave large candy bars on their front porch. The kids gather three or four large packets of Charmin and throw it upward in the front-yard trees of the ungenerous homeowner. The toilet paper tends to fall off the branches in flowing white lines that generally disappear in a few days. In my time, it was a badge of honor to have your front maple tree TP'd. It signified that you were a character and may actually have some people who envied you.

The other more vile prank was to egg a house. This practice was generally reserved for the owners of larger mansions who probably vacated their expensive domiciles for a winter in Palm Beach. "Oh, yeah! Let's get on the yacht!" For such globe-trotters, a dozen eggs thrown against the brick frontage of the house would remind the owners—or more likely, their service staff—that this ritual of cleaning the edifice was the price of affluence.

By the time Luis and his buddies reached their late teens, it was perhaps time to give up on this child-wonder holiday. But as one approaches his early twenties, Halloween ironically becomes a huge young adult celebration holiday, perhaps always accompanied by too many alcoholic drinks and strange costumes that protect one's anonymity and also by the macabre associations of the strange holiday. On this particular weekend, Eddie "became" the ghost. One of his friends costumed himself as a skeleton. Another as a wizard.

It was only an accident of timing that the boys were not incarcerated. It was only 7:00 p.m when the kids were driving down Lindell Boulevard and waving to strangers from the family late-model Ford. Then the police lights began to trail them. Within twenty-five yards, the car stopped, and the four participants in the car were asked to walk to the right and left of the vehicle (in costume) and were interrogated for several hours about their alleged attempts to harass the big homes on Hortense Place. All boys denied it, at least on this particular year.

After two months, there was no apparent evidence on the part of the Saint Louis Police department. (And make no mistake, this department is more than prone to find transgressions, especially with young men in ghost costumes, wizards, and other demented crazies in the car.) However, the young guys all willingly took and passed Breathalyzer tests, and there were no clear eggings of the luxury mansions in the Central West End.

Truth be told, it was just a bit too early in the evening for the young men to create their mischief. Consequently, they were completely exonerated.

However, once the dark deeds are in one's system, many do not wish to abandon it.

Perhaps that's why Luis and his buddies decided to visit San Antonio, Texas, the next year to revel in the ugly, scary costumes and the permission to sin on All Souls' Day." But as Eddie liked to privately admit many years later, it was always relatively harmless to walk toward the edge of danger, depravity, and dastardly deeds. The next year, he his friends would visit naughty New Orleans, and they hoped to escape this triple threat of disaster.

In years to come, they vowed to up the ante and visit the major macabre sites in the world:

1. The oceanic locale of the *Titanic* disaster

2. Normandy

3. The Haiti earthquake epicenter

4. Hurricane Michael's landfall point, Mexico Beach, Florida

5. The Hawaii volcanoes

That was the plan at that point. However, as young men get older, they may become more tender. They may have little munchkins of their own, make pumpkin soup for them, and walk the kids around the block in Casper the Friendly Ghost costumes. Along the way, they will look for the supersized candy bars and undoubtedly recall the off-center early memories of their more daring exploits.

32

When Lightning Strikes

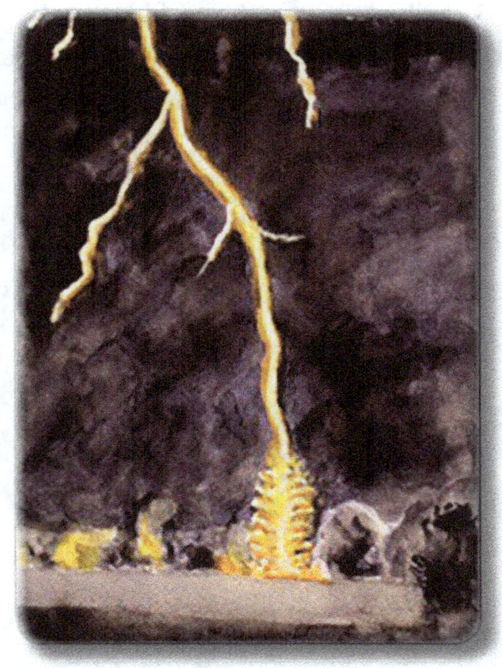

I know, it's not a child. Or a wife. Or a pet. It's just a damn tree.

But for many years, the one-hundred-year oak was a centerpiece of our front yard and source of entertainment for all the children who lived at this address. Often, they would climb up the strong branches. When the kids reached middle school age, my wife and I installed a stable swing on one of its branches. At first it was just for our children, but in time many neighborhood kids would sit on the wooden seat and rock back and forth.

For a while, I was worried about lawsuits if one of the neighbors got hurt. But the swing was only a foot or two from the ground. And what was I going to do? Put up a sign that advised that no neighbor kids would be allowed to be near the tree without a parent signing a legal release?

The tree even had a name: Woody. Not the most original moniker, but it made the attraction more personal for all participants. "I'm gonna get some fresh air, Dad, swinging on Woody," young James would say. "I'll be out by Woody," Tara would often suggest. Sometimes I would do the same, as would my wife.

So in some weird way, Woody was part of the family. As a hundred-year specimen, I took pride in the fact that it also functioned as a front-yard living anchor for four large families that had lived in our house before us. It didn't take too much imagination to visualize all these families enjoying the seasonal attraction of our front yard marvel. I could see snowball fights by the trunk in the middle of winter. I could envision prior families giggling at the spring leaves and falling into the orange-red autumn piles at the base of Woody.

So the tree had outlasted the roof, the windows, and most of the plants in the front yards and backyards. To be honest, I figured it would outlast my family and bring enjoyment to at least several other families long after we had moved on.

Such was not the case. In the midst a very bad weather forecast in 2016, the sky got very dark and the wind howled. All of us gathered in the basement for safety. I was worried about the devastating winds of a possible hurricane, and we lost all power in the home. Fortunately, we had a radio that advised us that only rare tornadoes were in the region. Given this scare, we hunkered down even further.

It sounded like a bombing. All our kids were screaming. My wife and I did our best to comfort them from the mysterious outside dangers. Within an hour or two, things subsided, and we all got up in the dark to see the damage that must have been inflicted on our dear home.

When we walked outside, it was eerily still. As we ventured out the front door, we discovered that the centerpiece of our front yard was burned to the stake.

Woody was dead. The once-beloved swing was now twenty yards away to the right of what remained as a dark scorched tree trunk. I admit to underestimating my children's reaction to this devastation. They immediately screamed to the heavens and ran into their mother's outreached hands. After thirty minutes of sobbing, I promised them we would have a proper burial and reincarnation of Woody.

The burial had to happen during the days when the kids were at school.

After all, it's a mulching of dead bark and transportation in a truck that delivers this debris who knows where.

But the ceremony for Woody was so much easier to arrange and was a family affair. In the same ground where the grand oak tree thrived, we planted a new sibling and said a private prayer for all that Woody had provided for so many families over one hundred years. As I closed my eyes and looked to the heavens, I hoped that this new oak tree could provide as much inspiration as its earlier progenitor.

33

If It Bleeds, It Leads–Or Maybe Not

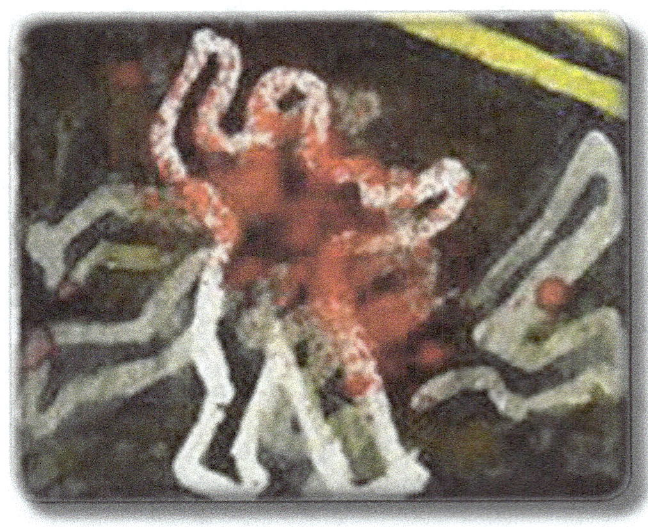

Mitch Coryell has been a reporter for the *New York Post* for the past thirty years. In that span, he has covered the horror of 9/11, the gory West Side bike path incident when a disgruntled truck driver decided to run over six Argentine bicyclists on a supposed holiday, and that atrocious stabbing attack of Timothy Caughman by a white supremacists.

Of course, in a city of 8.3 million people, there are more tragedies every single day. An unhappily married man kills his wife and the mother of his three children. A drunken driver unfortunately kills his best friend in a highway incident. An unhinged employee decides to kill his boss at Chase Manhattan in front of hundreds of witnesses. Such are the stories in the Naked City.

And such are the headlines of the *New York Post*. As James Johnson, Jr. the sixty-something managing editor of the newspaper would announce as he walked through the smoky newsroom of the busily typing haven of hell, he would often announce, "If it bleeds, it leads… so make it good. Make it convincing. Dramatize the human tragedy." After his advice, he would often smile at his employees. "I'll be in my office for the next forty-five minutes.

Think of a headline," he advised.

Over the past several decades, Mitch had written some of the *New York Post's* most clever headlines:

STUDENT EXCITED DAD GOT HEAD JOB

CHICK ACCUSES SOME OF HER MALE COLLEAGUES OF SEXISM

PORN STAR SUES OVER REAR-END COLLISION

12 SECRETARIES CLOBBERED IN BUSINESS BROUHAHA

MOM COMPLAINS THAT HER KIDS HAVE BEEN AXED BY HER EX

MURDER IN THE WELL-DRESSED STREETS OF GAY CHELSEA RESTAURANTEUR

Some of these gems would occasionally get complaints from readers of the flashy tabloid. More often, they would simply gain publicity and sell more copies. Occasionally the words would embarrass Mitch's teenage daughter.

"Dad, do you always need to do some sexual double-entendre with every headline?" she once asked her father.

"Not always." He shrugged. "Maybe I'll start writing sweet headlines," he said, laughing. "Of course, no one will read them."

He would soon have his chance to find out. After forty-three years at the editorial helm of the New York Post, his boss, James Johnson retired and appointed Mitch Coryell the new managing editor. Everyone at the famous newspaper thought it was a wise refocus. Some of the younger writers particularly wondered if the rag had become almost a parody of itself with its nonstop slasher headlines.

Of course, Mitch had heard these complaints for years. So he decided that given his new seat of power at the paper, he may as well try a limited experiment.

In a memo to his writing staff, he proposed a Happy Monday edition. It would be just for that one day of the week, while the other six days of publication would continue on its current sensational headline approach.

The experiment began with a cover story about the Girl Scout cookie- selling season. The headline? GIRL SCOUTS TAKE A BITE OUT OF CAPITALISM.

The next week, the paper covered the volunteers at retirement homes in the area, headline: HELP WANTED. HELP GIVEN.

There were other stories about advancements in cancer treatments, life expectancy, and minimum wage. There was also a ton of criticism from readers and from broadcast pundits who accused the New York Post of going soft. Subscriptions began to decline. Ad revenues on the Happy Monday editions decreased.

With absolutely no fanfare, Mitch ended the experiment. He called his staff together weeks later and announced, "Good news! We are returning to our tried-and-true format every day of the week. As my predecessor used to say, 'If it bleeds, it leads.' So go out there and find some stories people want to read and write some sensational headlines."

The next morning edition covered a multiple car crash with six fatalities on the George Washington Bridge. The headline: BANG. BANG. YOU'RE DEAD, TIMES 6.

There was no looking back. As the commentators on TV news smiled and said, "The Post is back! And most New Yorkers are quite happy to have this incredible source of our daily grind where it belongs—in our hands."

34

Keeping the Faith

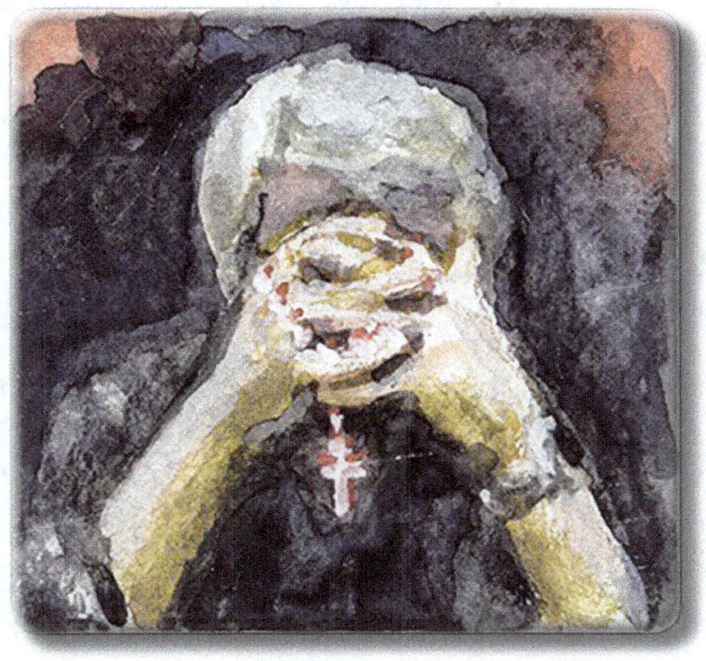

Jack Conner was no longer a particularly devout Catholic, especially when it came to Church rules and rituals. True, he had gone to a parochial school as a young boy and went to mass every weekday. He went to Notre Dame in college, married in the church, and baptized his two kids. But since that time, he basically described himself as a "cafeteria Catholic." In other words, "I'm OK with this, but disagree with that precept or that teaching."

For a while he would go to church on Easter and Christmas, but even those rituals began to fade as the man entered his forties. Like millions of Americans, he had just become too busy spend an hour in a pew praying.

Today was different.

Actually, the entire week was different. On Monday his only son Owen had a horrible motorcycle wreck that resulted in the amputation of both legs. For the first few days, the young man was completely unconscious. When he gained some drug-induced awareness of what had happened, Owen screamed loud enough for every patient in the ward to hear. His dad, who had held vigil all week, was holding his son's hand and crying.

The old man tried to force a smile. "We've got a long road ahead of us," Mr. Conner quietly said.

The young man shook his head. "A long, miserable, painful road," he said.

"Let's take it one day at a time," the dad advised.

Over the next several days, the young man faded in and out of awareness.

When he did become conscious, he would often writhe in pain and cry. It was awful, his dad believed. "I don't want this," the young boy repeatedly told his father.

The doctors advised that his recovery would be an ordeal, including a lifetime of drugs and psychotherapy. Of course, they were cheerleaders, but the son sighed with exasperation. "I don't want this," he told the doctors, and he then looked at his father.

The next afternoon, Mr. Conner went to Saint Agnes Church for the first time in a decade. Out of practice, he didn't quite know how to pray. He thought of wishing for a full recovery. No, that was too miraculous. How about a regenerated, redirected life for his son? Even that felt too ambitious.

Finally, he prayed that his son would no longer be in such pain.

After a rosary, Jack Conner returned to the hospital and was told that his son had just expired. The doctors seemed mystified and explained that his son simply stopped breathing and closed his eyes. "It was peaceful," the head surgeon said.

The father asked for some time with his son. He held the young man's hand, and between tears, he did feel some relief that Owen would no longer suffer.

Not surprisingly, the event did change Mr. Conner's life. To commemorate the event, he returned to church that one day every year and said the rosary.

As he told God, he was thankful that his prayers were answered and that his son ascended to heaven.

35

The Polar Bear Club

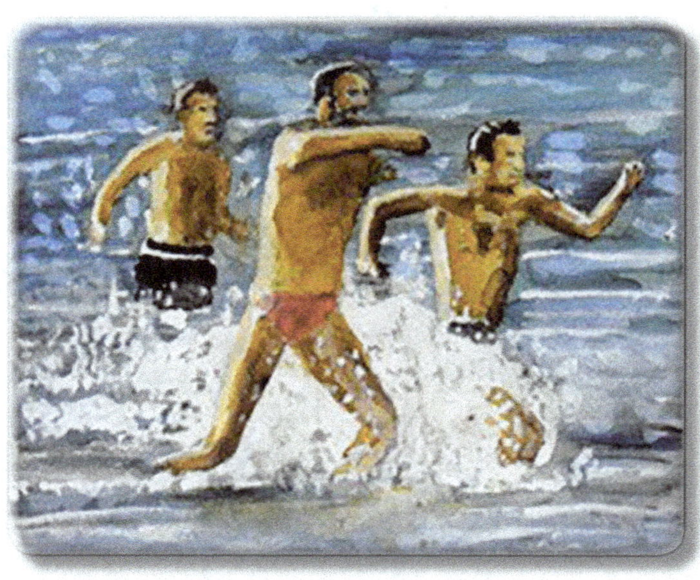

It's nothing you can actually train for. As a matter of fact, it's not really an athletic event. It's more of a dare, really—when thousands of people, usually with friends, descend on Coney Island on January 1 and strip down to their swimming squeezers, bikinis, or boxers and dive into the freezing Atlantic Ocean just to prove they can.

Jack Morehead had decided he wanted to give it a try. He enlisted a few buddies—Scott Jacobson and Peter Alverez—to try to stunt with him.

"It will be a rare, exceptional experience," Jack coaxed his friends. "Hopefully, a once-in-a-lifetime experience," Peter advised with an eye roll.

All three guys were in the midtwenties and were not graduates of their college swim teams. Ironically, they were not even into winter sports. True, they would occasionally go skiing, but hey, you can insulate yourself with layers of quilted materials and grab a brandy after a few runs to warm the innards of your soul.

On this particularly January 1, the temperature in New York hovered around twenty degrees. When the three friends compared notes at eight in the morning, they persuaded one another to take the plunge. It would be at least an hour commute from Manhattan, and they reminded themselves that they should bring a change of warm clothes and a camera. Evidently, they were expected to arrive at Coney Island by 11:00 a.m. to register for a charitable donation. With a twenty-five-dollar contribution, they could help raise almost $100,000 for charitable nonprofits on Coney Island.

In teeth-shattering freezing weather, the three guys waited online to help contribute to this 114-year tradition. (As an aside, this is also a legit winter club that features winter swimming in the Atlantic from November to April. How crazy is that?)

When the registrar asked the trio if they wished to join the all-winter-long organization, it was met with hilarious laughter from the three guys. Instead, they simply contributed twenty-five dollars each to the cause and then shivered their way away from the welcome desk.

They were amazed at the crowd. It was at least 40 percent women. At was at least 20–25 percent people in the later years—meaning for this cohort, fifty-plus. "Do you think they return year after year?" Jack Morehead asked his friends.

"God, I hope not," Peter Alverez riposted.

The *tick-tock* to the actual plunge was memorable for all three buddies.

They were expected to dive into the freezing water at 1:00 p.m. after a meet at Stillwell Avenue.

At that time, they were expected to strip down from their street clothes and get into swim gear. At least a hundred people to their right and left were instructed to do the same. Most participants stared at one another in anticipation.

Yes, it was cold to be stripped to your skivvies, but as several of the young men said, it was endurable. And then the whistle blew, and all participants knew they had to approach the icy water and dive into it until they were fully wet. That only takes about thirty seconds. The more excruciating part is to paddle their way back to the shore, which would take another forty-five seconds to a minute depending on your strokes. It was cold in the Atlantic Ocean. But it was even colder getting to the shore and exiting the ocean with icicles on the shivering body. Hopefully, if one remembers his embarking point, he can find his clean, oversized towel and dry clothing … and then wait in line by the restroom, shivering like mad, while waiting for a place to change into dry clothing.

With the lines of freezing strangers, it can take ten minutes. It's a small and large consolation. Yes, the participants are at least in some comfort. They have shed their wet, frozen clothing and can heave a sigh of relief. And yet it is an achievement. Such a small percentage of Americans ever choose to challenge such conditions.

"I feel so alive." Peter Alverez surprised the group with his optimism. Of all the buddies, and as a man of the Caribbean, this could not possibly be his cup of tea.

"Care to do it again next year?" Scott asked.

Jack looked at his two adventurous buddies. Both chimed in. "Not for me.

Maybe next year, we go to Jackson Hole and enjoy a brandy after a double black diamond run."

36

I Believe

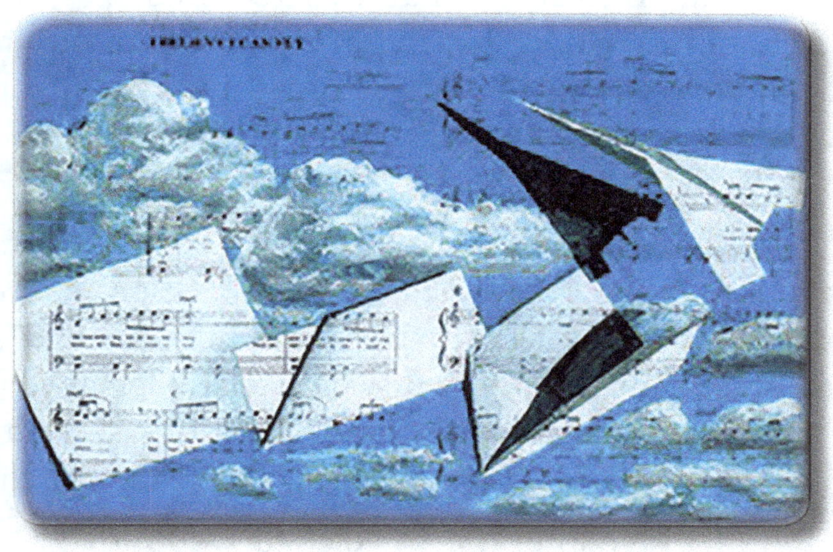

There is a posted sign near the small airstrip in Salina, Kansas. It reads *Skydiving is a high-risk activity which may cause or result in serious injury or death.*

Despite the fact that was three feet above his eye level, Chuck Palmer was able to read it. He fully understood the warning, winked at his instructor and signaled thumbs-up. He then wheeled himself into the terminal.

He had been preparing for this event for many months and had signed all the release forms weeks in advance. However, there is nothing like the actual moment of truth. Half the cadre of similar thrill seekers had already nervously gathered in the terminal. The DC- 3 airplane was already fueled and was now undergoing its final checks. And the weather? Perfect for an initial jump. The early October morning was crisp and clear with a gentle four-knot breeze.

In some ways, the conditions reminded him of that October day six years ago that resulted in his paralysis. At the time, he had been a troop commander in Iraq. He was knocked off his feet by one of those improvised explosive devices along a deserted dirt road. The Kevlar body armor had evidently saved his life but could not prevent the T-1 injury to his spinal cord. The next year was a particularly challenging period for Palmer. There is no way to minimize the physical and mental adjustment that was required of him on a daily basis. However, he no longer had nightmares about the incident and had devoted his new life to moving forward instead of looking back. His recent college diplomas and teaching job were testaments to that progress. This activity, while purely recreational, would serve as a personal exclamation point.

Chuck's tandem partner and instructor, a man called Clarence Jackson, had fifteen years of jumping experience and had successfully accomplished many guided descents with paraplegics. He outfitted Palmer on the ground with an elaborate safety lock system around his legs and torso. He then looked at Palmer. "You ready for this?"

"I believe I am," the man in the wheelchair responded.

"Well, it's now or never." Clarence smiled back and transported him to the aircraft with the other first-timers.

The only real nerve-racking part was time spent waiting in the aloft plane.

Several of his fellow novices simply stared out the open window in silence before building the courage to leap. When it was Palmer's time, Clarence reminded him to arch his back as much as possible on the way down. And then they were off.

The actual free fall was the most exhilarating thirty seconds Chuck Palmer had ever experienced. The only sounds in the air were his moans of ecstasy.

Despite the high, he did have the presence of mind to survey the free blue sky and approaching farm fields. Wow.

Upon a gestured cue, Clarence pulled the rip cord, and the canopy opened flawlessly. This floating sensation was also almost as thrilling as hurtling through space. As they had rehearsed, Clarence leaned back for a balanced soft landing on his legs. Palmer could only think it was over too quickly.

There were the inevitable high fives with his instructor. There was champagne waiting for him in his truck. Throughout it all, Chuck was constantly beaming. Sure, it felt wonderful to jump. But in his case, it felt even better to know that he had just completed an activity that most people with four good limbs were afraid to ever attempt.

Back in the terminal, Clarence asked the first-timers if any of them wished to do it again next weekend. Most demurred. A few feebly raised their hands.

Chuck Palmer's arm was raised the highest.

"I believe I would," the young man said as he grinned. He had already filled out the release form for next week's jump. He folded once, twice, and then converted it to a paper airplane, which he sailed on the desk of Clarence Jackson. It was a perfect landing, just like the one he had just accomplished and would again achieve the following week.

37

The Not-So-Little Libation

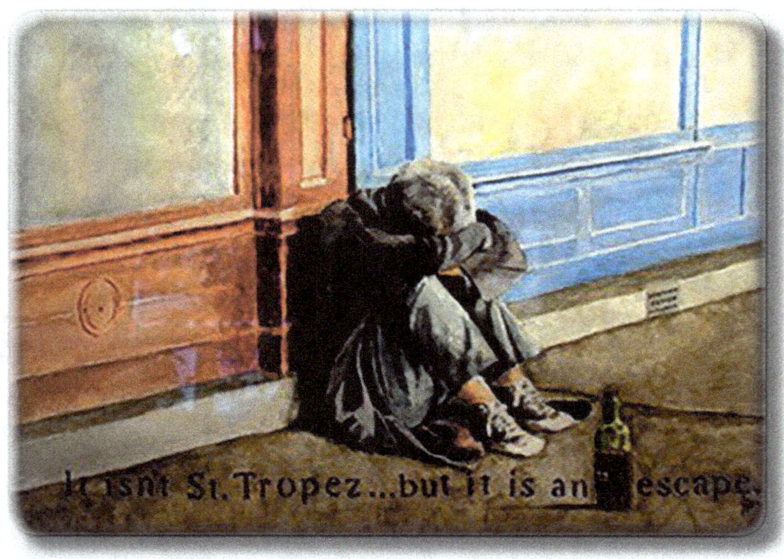

Marcel Sardou particularly enjoyed the springtime in Paris. The winters were a bit harsh for his comfort, and the summer always seemed to bring too many tourists. But the spring? There was always music in the air from the street buskers.

It reminded him of the days when he would sit in an outdoor café, flirt with the beautiful young women, and enjoy a midday glass of Bordeaux.

That was a long, long time ago. The days when he had worn a business suit and had money for a boeuf bourguignon were clearly now gone. So was his wife of eleven years. At the time, everyone thought they were the model couple—the smiling man and wife featured on all the wedding cakes.

Between his job as a publishing executive and hers as a fashion consultant, they had plenty of money to hobnob around the bright glitter spots of Europe.

That all changed on October 24 of 1999. They were out celebrating their anniversary at La Coupole. The meal was superb, and the wine poured freely.

However, on the way home he lost control of his Peugeot and accidentally rammed into a concrete bridge abutment. The entire right side of the sedan was crushed. While Marcel was injured, his beautiful wife was instantly knocked unconscious and was a bloody mess. He tried desperately to revive her, but she was completely unresponsive. By the time the ambulance arrived, she was pronounced dead.

Different people deal with grief in different ways. This widower took the turn of events in the worst possible way since he felt partly responsible for the tragedy. He would bounce around the apartment they once shared and cry himself to sleep. He often missed days at work and was eventually fired by Paris Match. And he began drinking too much. At first it was just a few glasses a day, but within a year he could easily quaff a bottle or more in an afternoon.

It would be tempting for Marcel to say that once drunk, he felt no pain. In fact, he did say so every day. His only refuge was that bottle of cheap Bordeaux. Occasionally, he would lift his head and look out from his sidewalk perch. Sometimes, he would see the beautiful couples walking by. They might be laughing or simply hugging romantically. For a flash, it would remind him of the life he once had. But normally, he would soon realize that he was just a spectator and would always be such. When that happened, it was time for another swig.

38

Hymn

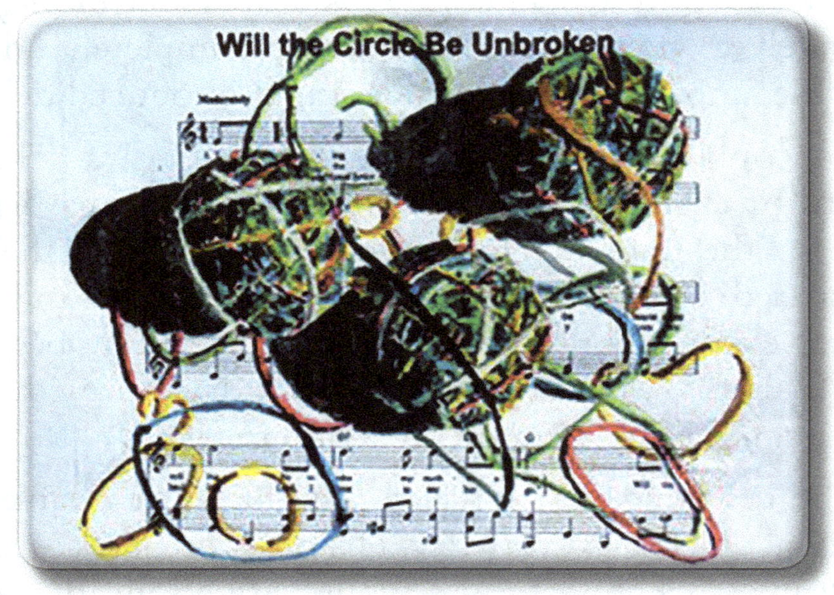

Jimmy Robertson was one of the most beloved folks in the small town of Byron Falls, Idaho. At heart, he was an entertainer and clown. In fact, he performed kid parties for the past fifty years—in homes, parks, and even the Good Shepherd Church basement, where kids of all ages would watch his magic at least once a month after the service.

Often he would juggle balls made of rubber bands, and at the end of his show, he would pass a few of them out to some young members of the audience. Over the decades, many of the townsfolk had these rubber band souvenirs from his shows. Even the preacher at Good Shepherd had one, as a memento of Jimmy Robertson's sunny disposition.

Unfortunately, that positive influence was now interrupted. Jimmy had just passed of old age, and his casket rested in the center aisle of this funeral mass. The church was packed with people who wanted one last interaction with the showman.

As the preacher recounted Jimmy's long-lasting power, he took a ball of bound rubber bands and carefully untangled a strand. With his index finger, he stretched a lone red band several inches and asked his congregation the questions that consume each of us in this life. "Will this life break us? Will we have the flexibility move forward? Will our time here on earth be the end? Or will we ultimately be connected to a more glorious life in heaven?"

As was usually the case, the congregation joined in affirmation, agreeing with the preacher's leading questions. As they did so, the organist began to play the familiar hymn.

There are loved ones in the glory

Whose dear forms we often miss.

When you close your earthly story,

Will you join them in the bliss?

Will the circle be unbroken?

By and by, by and by?

Is a better home awaiting?

In the sky, in the sky?

The congregation applauded their own performance, as they had often done for Jimmy's shows. The preacher then brought out a box of bound rubber-band balls and tossed them to everyone who had attended. As a final coda, the organist reprised the familiar chorus, and the churchgoers happily sang, "Will the circle be unbroken?"

39

The Sexiest Newscaster in America

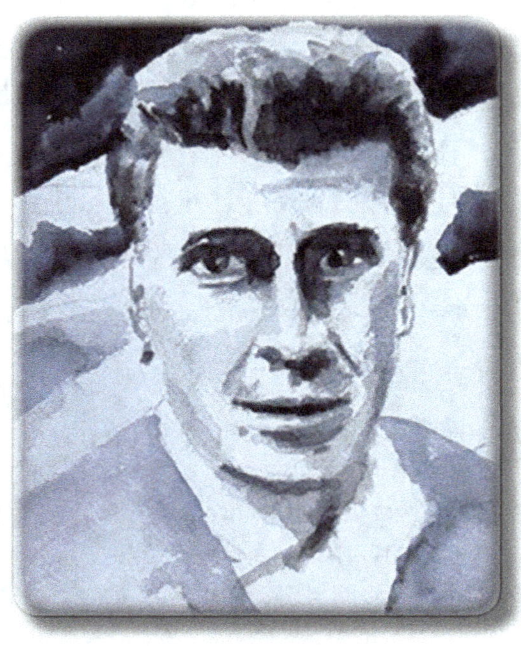

Perhaps you remember Rhett Reynolds, that hunk from NBC News, who was dubbed the Sexiest Newscaster in America by *People* magazine in 1994. That was, of course, before it became totally unacceptable to comment on a man's or woman's looks. It, of course, preceded the #MeToo movement that brought down Charlie Rose, Marc Halpern, Matt Lauer, Bill O'Reilly, Les Moonves … Ah, the list goes on and on.

However, at the time, such cute teasing headlines were fair game for both genders. Katie Couric was called "America's sweetheart." Megyn Kelly was often referred to as "the hottest anchor on cable news." Harris Faulkner of Fox News is still referred to as "Va-va-va-voom."

But the preoccupations with looks has definitely diminished in the past ten years. Part of this is President Trump's irresponsible comments on the bus about grabbing women by the genitalia. A bigger part has definitely been the lawsuits against men in power, including Bill Cosby and Harvey Weinstein.

And then came the avalanche of negative publicity!

At the ripe age of forty-five, Rhett Reynolds hoped he had perhaps outlived that era. In the past fifteen years, he had been a good man, as he liked to claim to his neighbors and media reporters. But the past is not always a forgotten bit of history. Sometimes, it's a prelude to the here-and-now.

In a recent deposition, his secretary accused him of reaching up her skirt in a private meeting fourteen years ago. His executive assistant accused him of coming out of his private shower in a sexually aroused state. Most crippling, several screen stars (including some Oscar winners) accused him of inappropriate behavior. Once it starts, the floodgates open. New accusations come out of the woodwork.

Eventually, Roger Ailes, the now beleaguered CEO of Fox news, placed the popular anchor on a six-month leave of absence.

In the next six months, Ailes was asked by the board of directors to resign, and Rhett Reynolds was on every tabloid in America as a sex pervert. During that period, he was approached by dozens of news magazines to give his side of the story.

As his lawyer advised him, it would be easy to rebut the accusations, but it would be presumable fruitless. As his ex-wife advised him, "In this environment, with anyone who is as good-looking as you … Well, people want to believe that despite your good looks, you must be a prick!"

After some months of trying to deny the accusations, Rhett gave up. With the advice of his agent, he decided to reinvent himself as a reformed person.

Step 1 was to release a tell-all book. He decided to feature his most attractive Hollywood picture on the front of the book and title it *The Sexiest Lost Soul.*

Perhaps you know that it reached number 107 on the best-seller list, was panned by all the critics, and then quickly faded. So did Rhett, who for the past seven years in his now anonymous life, has sorely missed the notoriety.

As he recently revealed in the *People* magazine "Where Are They Now?" article, "This obscurity may as well be death."

40

Happy Birthday, Anyone

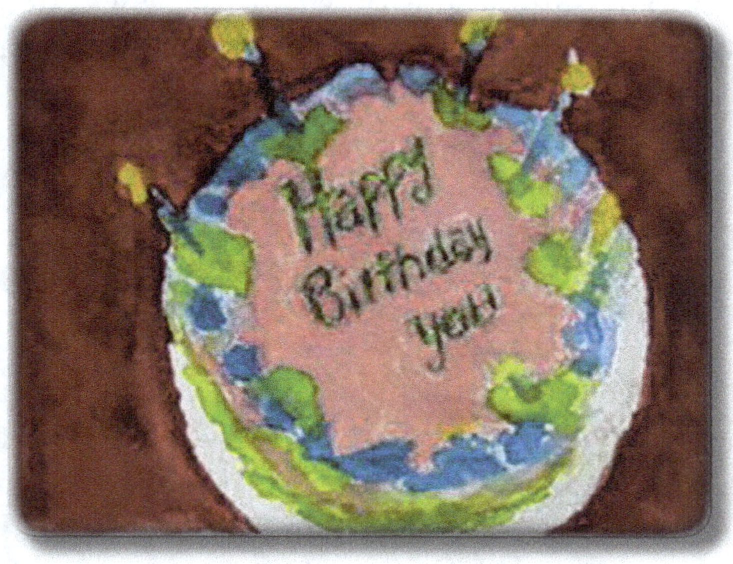

One month after her mother's death, Jenna Ortiz enrolled in the Institute of Culinary Education. It had been a very sad several weeks, since the elder Mrs. Ortiz was taken with a stroke and expired in the next few days. The whole rigmarole of arranging a funeral as an only child was daunting. First of all, there are all those details that most of us are unaccustomed to coping with. More to the point, there is that severe sadness. Unfortunately, in the whirlwind of funeral arrangements, there is almost no time to grieve. Once her mother had her burial, Jenna did cry and wanted never again to feel so down.

Her immediate solution was to get busy with distractions. Always a wiz in the kitchen, she enrolled in a few recreational classes at Sur La Table. From past experience, she found these exercises to be tonic for all the worries of the world. It's just enough mental, physical, and artistic endeavors to take your mind off the troubles of the world. On this particular week, she took a class in Thai cuisine and one in cheesecake making. She preferred the latter and always did favor sweets over savory. As she liked to tell her friends, "These days, everyone sends every dish back to the kitchen for more salt, less peanuts, or more 'doneness.' No one ever sends a dessert back. Hey, if you don't want tiramisu, don't order tiramisu!"

Consequently, she enrolled in the bakery program at ICE. From day 1, she enjoyed the experience. First of all, it's a small class setting—with about fifteen students, most of whom get switched around every week, according the instructor's whim. Every day has a new menu, and groups are assigned to work as a team. And there are cuisines to be learned—bread making, custards, cookies, pies, cakes, decorating, ice creams and gelatos, French desserts, Italian specialties, etc., etc., etc. Jenna endured the class on bread making but particularly enjoyed the cake baking, and she seemed to have a special affinity for cake decorating.

One of the nicer things about a class such as this is that the students get to bring back the overflow of their work. True, at the end of the class, every student tastes every dish from every group, but there is always more than enough for the fifteen students. Consequently, all of Jenna's friends were always treated to desserts every night!

At the completion of her curriculum, this Blue Ribbon graduate got an externship job at Lady M Cake Boutique on the Upper Side of Manhattan— an establishment with an excellent reputation for mille crepes, green tea checkered cakes, and pumpkin nudge. Like most bakeries, the hours are ungodly. Normally, the baking staff arrives around three in the morning so that all the cakes and pastries can be baked fresh every day. Not surprisingly, the smell in the kitchen is a high for every worker. While the opening hours are harsh, the closing hours are quite generous. Most bakers leave by three in the afternoon (or earlier) and thereby leave the sale of baked goods for the sales staff at the place.

Jenna worked at the establishment for one year, and she felt she was well treated by management. However, she had bigger plans. She missed baking cakes and cake decorating. Also, on this anniversary of her mother's death, she missed her mother. On the heels of this sad milestone, Jenna decided to create an even happier path. She searched out vacant bakeries and found one in her near vicinity that was relatively affordable. In view of her affirmative attitude, she named it "Happy Birthday from Jenna." It would feature cookies, biscottis, breads, muffins, but mostly birthday cakes beautifully decorated by Jenna and her staff with handwritten messages. Often they are creative cakes, sometimes intentionally lopsided, and often with gooey, gushy ingredients. Recently, in *Westchester Magazine*, it was voted the most creative birthday cake place in the county.

Sometimes, Jenna and her staff have twenty-five birthday cakes to create and inspire over a weekend. They never miss. In her heart, "It's the most wonderful job in the world to me—so many people happy so many times every year." She's been doing it now for ten years after her mother's death.

It's been a good decade of positive thinking. However, on this particular anniversary, she created an inscription on a small cake that said "Happy Birthday, Momma." In the isolation of her apartment, Jenna took a bite, was thankful for her mother's influence, and ultimately smiled at her good fortune to bring joy to people.

41

Stop, Dammit

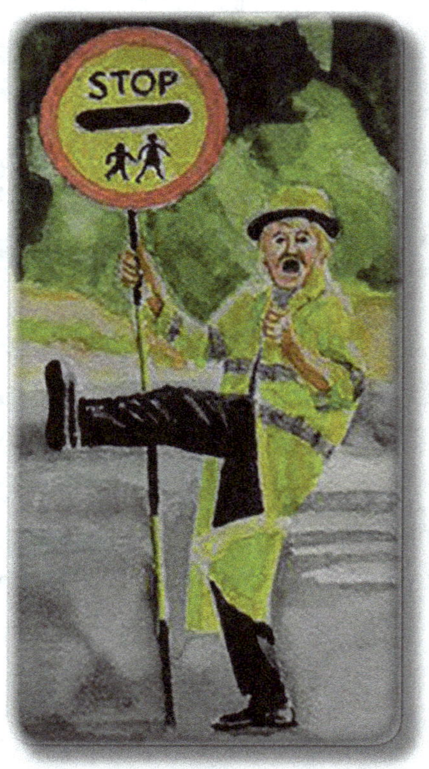

Lucy Middleton has been doing the job for the past thirty years and has increasingly felt that everyone was in a hurry get across the street and race through her stop signs. "It's dangerous," she told her local newspaper who had profiled her in a recent article.

The story and puff piece revealed that, decades ago, she had raised four children in the school district and held her breath every day they walked to and from school. "I felt the kids were safe in school, but on the streets? Who knows?" Consequently, she applied to the village of Irvingon, New York, to be a school crossing guard every morning on behalf of child safety.

A big part of the job is cautioning the school children to *not* cross the intersection before her signal to "walk now." The bigger part of her job is to enhance the awareness of the very busy, cell-phone obsessed drivers who are increasingly ignorant of what's in front of them, whether it be a six-year-old child or a ninety-two-year-old woman in a walker. Over the past few years, she has added frantic pantomime and dance routines to capture the attention of the drivers and encourage them to hit their brakes.

"I sometimes think the drivers must consider themselves very, very important people who must somehow get to their destination ASAP. I am reluctant to tell you how many close calls happen at my intersection on Broadway, especially in the afternoons, when drivers seem particularly rushed."

"Ever witnessed an accident on that intersection?" the reporter asked.

Lucy knocked on the wooden desk and gave a sigh of relief. "So far, so good," the eighty-year-old woman responded.

That luck was about to change. On November 18, right before the Thanksgiving break, Lucy was holding up traffic while the third graders were dismissed from school at 2:45 p.m. This is the trickiest time, since the kids come in waves and traffic backs up a little. From experience, Lucy has learned to have the kids wait, wait, wait, and then proceed across the crosswalk in groups of twenty to twenty-five kids. She then waves three to four cars through while asking the next group of kids to wait, wait, wait.

While the kids are huddled by the sidewalk, she then holds up her stop sign and does her antics in the middle of the street to persuade the motorists to yield to pedestrians. Evidently, on this particular afternoon, a certain Carl Benton was too busy with his cell phone to see her cha-cha in the middle of the street. *Fwack!*

The 2012 Buick sped toward the octogenarian grandma and crossing guard. It knocked her off her feet and splayed her on the asphalt. Fortunately, she was not knocked unconscious, but she did suffer some leg injuries (including a broken hip). Several kids waiting by the sidewalk immediately pulled out their cell phones and called 911. In one positive sign, the driver did not speed away but remained on the site to make sure the woman was cared for with an ambulance. BTW, those young kids on the sidewalk were well trained. Many wrote down the license number of the driver just in case he decided to speed away. Ahh, young witnesses!

Over the Christmas holiday season, many of the kids and their parents brought flowers to the local hospital, where Lucy was recovering from hip surgery. In the beginning of the year, the local reporter did another feature on the village's favorite crossing guard (who had been replaced for months with local cops and volunteers). According to Lucy, she was just "most thankful that the car struck her instead of the kids." The guy driving the Buick has a day in court, but that's months away. He was in tears at the scene of the accident and actually did help load Lucy into the ambulance. Perhaps he will get a lighter sentence, if he agrees to get rid of his cell phone.

Lucy Middleton now walks with a brace. She goes to physical therapy two to three times a week. Hopefully, by next September, she will be spry as ever and back on her familiar crosswalk, hugging the kids again, and doing that cha-cha of hers in the middle of street, perhaps for one more year.

Meanwhile, she has added a very loud whistle to her daily equipment.

42

Hurricane Waffle

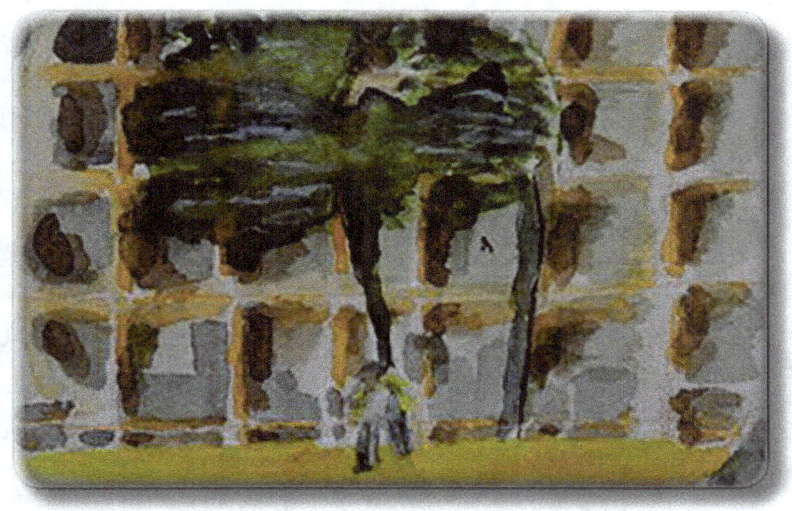

The newscasts in Fort Pierce had predicted disaster. "Hurricane Michael is on its way! We recommend that everyone within my speaking voice board up the windows and evacuate in the next twenty-four hours!"

Mitch Gates had already begun that process in his small family home. Fact is, he had the boards in his garage from past storms. In every case, he and his wife had avoided disaster (or broken glass), but as Mitch liked to caution his wife and kids, "Better safe than sorry."

He let everyone know that he had booked a small hotel 160 miles away, closer to the Georgia border, and he informed his wife and three kids that they should all be prepared to leave by 9:00 a.m.

"I'm going to ride it out in the house," his eighteen-year-old son, Gary, stated matter-of-factly.

"Excuse me?" his dad reacted.

"Dad, the last three hurricanes have been mild. Besides, I want to feed the cat, and I have to work this weekend."

"Work in a hurricane?" Mr. Gates scoffed.

"Dad, it's the Waffle House tradition! We are open twenty-four hours a day, 365 days a year. Indeed, it has been a badge of courage since Hurricane Hugo in 1989. In the ensuing years, the restaurant has endured ten hurricane responses in the past seventeen years. Where else are the crews and emergency workers going to get food?"

"It's just a macho thing!" Mitch protested.

"We prefer to call it a bravery thing," young Gary answered. "And what if someone gets hurt?"

"We all sign releases," the son answered smugly.

That just made the caring dad feel even worse. However, if you have an eighteen-year-old, you might know it is difficult to boss them around like a young child. They do have a mind of their own, and as parents, we generally applaud that. After more contretemps, Brad reluctantly laid out some rules.

"You should stock up on food. If it gets bad, you should sleep upstairs. If it gets really bad, you should sleep in the tub. If you lose power, hug the cat, so she doesn't get freaked out. How will you get to the Waffle House?"

"If the roads are flooded, I can walk. I've got those fly-fishing boots."

The next morning, Gary helped his dad, mom, and two sisters load the car. At the door of the Jeep, he gave his dad a big hug and promised he would be very careful, feed the cat, and keep his cell phone fully charged as long as there was power. The hug felt like a college or military goodbye, but the eighteen-year-old reminded himself that it would hopefully only be a few days of separation.

That afternoon, Gary walked to the Waffle House and did his usual eight- hour shift. It was uneventful, other than the fact that his manager gave him a key fob with a list of relevant numbers. He was also given a giant binder labeled "In Case of Hurricanes." The manager did announce that six employees would be evacuating and were being replaced with a jump team— a group of volunteers who work in place of locals in climactic catastrophes.

It's almost like a SWAT team of wafflers.

That night, the storm began to hit Fort Pierce. As Gary watched the news with his cat, Boo-boo, he stroked her to lessen her skittishness. According to the newscasters, the velocity of wind would pick up after midnight—up to 120 miles per hour. It's not like a gas pedal on your car that slowly increases mph. It comes in gusts. These sudden eruptions are why windows break and roofs disengage. It's also extremely noisy. Very much like a war.

At 4:00 a.m., the house went dark. At four fifteen, Gary was stumbling around the house with a flashlight, calling out "Boo-boo, Boo-boo." He couldn't find her, but he did set out cat food in four different locations on their second-floor sanctuary.

At 7:00 a.m., when Gary walked on the mostly destroyed front porch, he assessed the damage from the earlier night. It affected most of the homes in his neighborhood.

Trees were upended. Cars were overturned. Electrical lines were down. And then there was a rub on his leg—a furry rub and a purr from Boo-Boo. Instinctively, Gary picked up his dear cat and gave her the biggest hug of his life. He promptly walked her up the ramshackle stairs and made sure she had plenty of Meow Mix and water. After a half hour of affection, he called the numbers on the key fob and realized that his local Waffle House had limited service but welcomed all employees.

The eighteen-year-old negotiated the flooded streets and made blueberry waffles for the firefighters and rescue workers, thanks to the Waffle House generator.

That night, they still had the residual back stream of the Hurricane Michael.

It wasn't quite as bad as the initial hit, but once again, it did sound like a train wreck on the house. That afternoon, Gary served at the Waffle House with the jump team from New Jersey, Missouri, Arkansas, and Colorado. It felt noble.

Once again, Boo-Boo was safe. That evening, he heard from his dad, his mom, and his three sisters.

Given the conditions, they were advised by Florida to avoid the highways until five days later. Of course, when they arrived, the house was a shocking disaster, However, it was restorable, especially by Mitch. But he was so thankful that his son had survived this most recent disaster.

The aftermath: In this devastating hurricane, seventeen people died.

Eight people perished in Florida.

It happens with every disaster, but that is not this story. Two months later, Mitch and his eighteen-year-old son were rebuilding the home in Fort Pierce.

Gary continued to work at the Waffle House but volunteered any off day to help his dad rehab the semi destroyed house. After several weeks, his father wondered, "Would you do that again?"

"You bet. I have already volunteered to be part of the Waffle House jump team. If people need us in North Carolina, Mississippi, Houston, New Orleans, Miami, or North Carolina, I will be there."

43

Tricks of the Trade

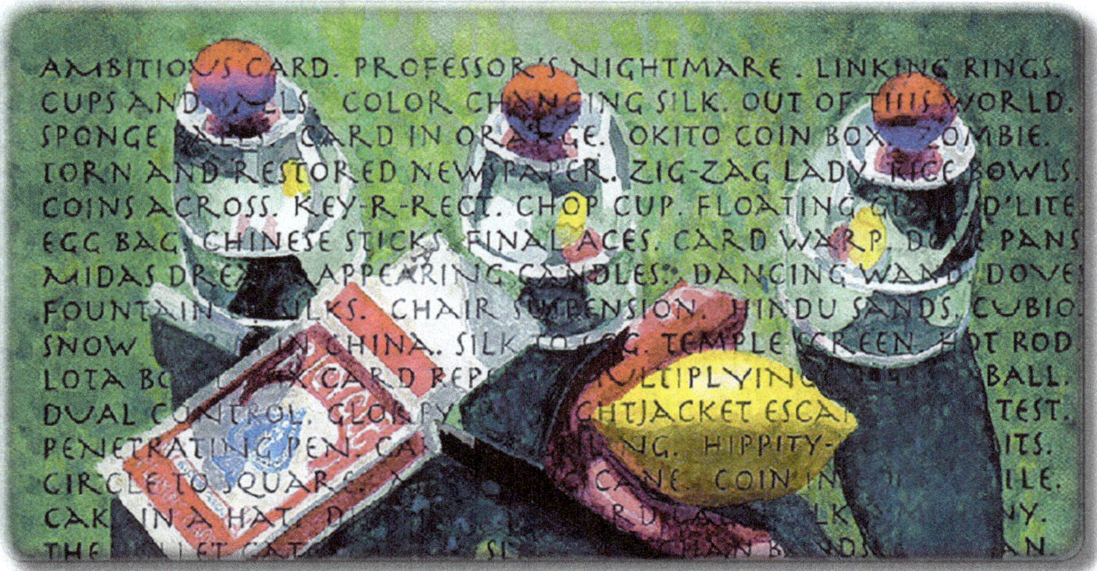

Few people at the Frank E. Campbell funeral home in Manhattan knew that Joe Campbell had a secret passion for magic. As the managing director and son of the somber founder, Joe fully understood that he had a persona to maintain, and it didn't include sleight of hand. His grieving customers expected decorum, comfort, and the professional reassurance that every detail in their time of need would be seamlessly handled in an above-board manner. For that reason, the magic tricks that amused Joe were safely stowed behind the desk in that Duncan Fife credenza. Inside a hidden drawer, he had his cups and balls, palming coins, and dozens of bicycle desks. On slow days, he would eat his bagged ham-and-cheese sandwiches inside his locked office and then practice the double lift and the classic pass. It tickled him. And in an environment with very few tickles, this hobby served as an oasis of personal sanity.

Joe was practicing the Elmsley count when he heard a knock on the door.

"Be right with you," he called out, and he quickly stashed the deck.

He assumed his concerned countenance and opened the door. It was an elderly woman who asked about the Campbell Funeral Home for her deceased husband, a man called Roberto Slydini.

"The Amazing Slydini," Joe reacted with a jolt. Like every amateur magician, the funeral director considered the man a hero ever since he created that multideck dazzler called Card King. "It would be an honor," Joe quickly added, and he spent the next thirty minutes discussing arrangements in his typical, consoling manner.

"There are two special requests," the widow added. "One, there should be a pack of cards in the casket. Two, this should be a true celebration of his life.

In parlor A, that you've suggested, there should be at least four close-up tables for all the magicians that will undoubtedly attend and pay their last respects with their own version of my late husband's best tricks."

"You want close-up tables near the casket?" "Roberto asked for it in his will," she answered.

Joe Campbell had heard unusual respects in his ten years at the helm of the establishment. Bereavements of Broadway legends sometimes included their musical hits. The services of a few famous politicians had occasionally included videos of their more celebrated speeches. But even with this history of customized arrangements, a bevy of close-up magic tables was unique. Joe looked at his business calendar and discovered there were no other services scheduled for the evening when Slydini would lie in state. "We can handle that," the director answered sympathetically.

It was a joyous event. Marco the Magnificent attended. So did Billdini. And the Great Carlos. In fact, at least one hundred world-famous magicians came. As the widow had predicted, they all lined up at the felt tables to display their favorite interpretations of Slydini's modern classics.

It was nearly impossible for Joe Campbell to resist participating in those fun close-up tables. However, the man did understand he had a different role to perform. As a funeral director, he had to be the very picture of the serious consoler.

Privately, he took immense pride in the fact that he had carefully placed his own deck of playing cards in the crossed hands of the Amazing Slydini. Just as thrilling, he surreptitiously circulated in the parlor and observed nine different astonishing variations of Card King.

Thirty minutes later, Mrs. Slydini gathered her thanks and said, "Thank you for making all this possible. Roberto would have been very pleased."

Joe Campbell excused all his employees and prepared to close the place.

For the first time in a decade, he mused, *What an absolutely great*

job I have. Also for the first time since he became director of the funeral home, he brought his hobby out in the open. In the dark privacy of parlor A, he reached into his breast pocket and took out a deck of cards. On the close-up table nearest to the casket of the Amazing Slydini, he then performed his own version of Card King in front of the master.

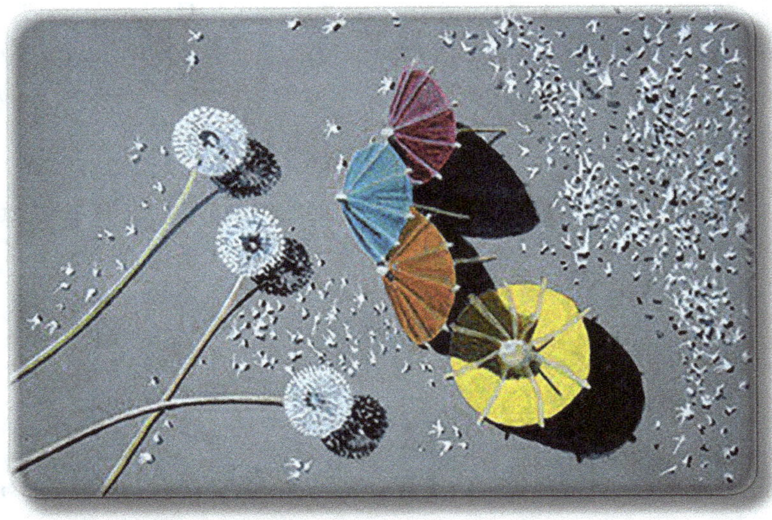

There are two things that Letitia Morganthal had always requested of her staff in Newport, Rhode Island.

1. Around 12:01 p.m., she loved to be surprised with a paper-parasol cocktail … or two or three. As William, her butler, had discovered morning, the timing was critical. (Once, he had mistakenly brought Morganthal a Negroni at 11:45 a.m., only to discover her are wrath "William, how dare you! Have you no sense of propriety? Have you wristwatch? It is far too early, too gauche, too vulgar for a woman society to imbibe an alcoholic libation at this hour!" When Will sheepishly put the Negroni on the serving tray, Ms. Morganthal quickly advised him to bring it back in sixteen minutes.)

By the way, she was not picky about the exact concoction. Truth be told, she preferred daiquiris in the summer. However, at this point in her life, there were so few movable parts that the "Surprise me" command was a welcomed bit of spontaneity. It could be a mai tai, a

Singapore sling, a blue Hawaii, a strawberry margarita, or any number of other fruity drinks.

As long as it came with a paper umbrella, Ms. Morganthal felt festive. She always demanded that her backyard facing the ocean be pristine green, i.e., no dandelions. As she often told her gardener, Francisco "People take the ocean walk to get a brief vision of the perfect life big ugly dandelion destroys that illusion." Admittedly, Leticia ha double standard in this regard. The young yellow dandelions could fact, be mowed. But the white, bulbous, seed- carrying stage? No way. "They are the dangerous, destructive, invasion ones, Francisco. T must be harvested before they spread their sperm across the law Consequently, the gardener's instructions were to pick those late sp carriers, contain them, and then discard them in weekly trash.

Other than those two provisos, it was a fairly easy mansion to work.

William and Francisco had been employees of the house for the past thirty years—ever since Leticia's rich husband had died and willed the entire estate to her. Neither domestic employee had attended the particular passage, but both had done so this morning for their just-deceased employer—Ms. Leticia.

According to probate lawyers, the Newport mansion would be sold and the proceeds would be donated to the Newport Historical Society. However, there was a jarring, pleasant surprise for both employees. Each was willed $1.5 million—more money than either expected—or even dreamed of earning in their lifetimes. It was a godsend. It was a jackpot. It was a potentially life-changing event.

Today, at eleven forty-five, the two shocked men were seated in Ms. Leticia's favorite patio, preparing to imbibe a generous assortment of Singapore slings, daiquiris, Negronis, and other cocktails. While William was preparing those parasol drinks, Francisco picked his last dandelions from the otherwise green yard facing the Atlantic and placed the white seed carriers on the table.

As the two men comforted themselves at the deserted mansion and viewed the Atlantic, there was a long silence. A few tourists paused along the Ocean Walk, and appeared to curiously fantasize about the two middle-aged men sitting in adjoining Adirondack chairs. The two inheritors royally waved at the passersby and shared a surreal appreciation for all that the old woman had bestowed upon them.

William looked at the TAG Heuer wristwatch Ms. Morganthal had once given him. "We should really wait until twelve-oh-one," he told his friend.

"I should really clean up those dandelion seeds." Francisco winced.

"They are flying everywhere. Bad for the lawn."

At 12:03 p.m., the two men toasted each other with sangrias and other umbrella drinks. Several hours later, after countless waves to the tourists on the Ocean Walk, the two men enjoyed their last sunset in the shadow of Ms. Morganthal's everlasting influence.

45

Paradise Lost

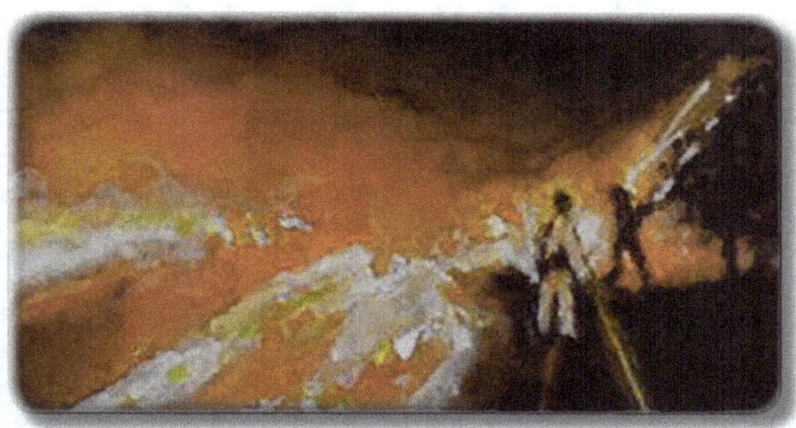

Like many idyllic parts of California, the town was named for the ultimate escape and perpetually happy state of affairs. At the time, the town folks considered calling it Nirvana but thought that was perhaps a tad too exotic. Instead, they named it Paradise, and thousands of retirees moved there from Michigan, Wisconsin, Missouri, and Pennsylvania in the hopes of Adam-and- Eve heaven. As many have discovered in the past week, that tenure was not intended to include the ugly fires of hell.

Jack Bernstein had moved west from Detroit, Michigan, after retiring from the nearby Bingham Farms Fire Department. He was a captain and had reached civil service retirement age, but with every passing day, he missed the community service. Consequently, when he moved to Paradise with his wife Wendy, he offered to volunteer for the local fire department.

"I spent thirty years in this field and don't wish to boss those around me.

But I miss the camaraderie of the fire department, and if you need an extra hand, I am willing to help."

"For free?" the Paradise police chief asked.

"I already have a pension," Jack answered. "This is just to make a contribution to my new community.

"Welcome aboard," the chief answered, and he took down all of Jack's vital information in case of vacations or sudden emergencies.

The first few months were pretty easy. He was called in for an apartment blaze while several firefighters were on vacation. All tenants were saved. He helped intercede on an auto crash that incinerated a car and the driver, but this was *de rigueur* in most fire departments. You save most people, but inevitably there are casualties.

However, despite his intense experience with disaster, he could not anticipate the latest California wildfire. The chief called him on Monday.

"Jack, we have an absolute emergency on our hands in the next twenty-four hours. Can you get to the station ASAP. It's all hands on deck." Given his proximity, he reached the firehouse in fourteen minutes. When he arrived, everyone was gathered around a large computer screen showing the genesis of the campfire, the wind conditions, and the prediction that flame would most likely reach Paradise by 9:00 a.m. the next morning.

Seeing this forecast, he immediately called his wife, Wendy, and urged her to grab a very few valuable things and evacuate their new dream home in the next few hours.

"By when?" she asked.

"Drive to Nevada before eight p.m. tonight. I must sleep in the firehouse and help the cause, but I want you to be safe."

After several "I love yous" the couple wished each other the very, very best along with even more "I love yous."

By six the next morning, all the firefighters were out of the house and on the way the encroaching firestorm just a few miles from Paradise, California.

They did their best to send water to all the trees, but with the howling winds, the flames jumped above all branches and began to ignite the community. Within a few hours, the fire trucks retreated to the southern part of the town.

By 9:00 p.m., it was another retreat. The alarm bells of disaster rang for seventy-two hours, but as everyone in the firehouse knew, it was hopeless.

Most homes were lost. Many people were missing in flames. At one point, Jack drove by his neighborhood and discovered that all the homes on his block were incinerated (including his and Wendy's new dream home). He wondered about the fate of his neighbors but instinctively knew that most would be lost unless they evacuated like his wife.

He did call Wendy that night to report on his safety and check in on her status in Nevada.

"The news reports are scary as can be," she opened up. "Are you safe and sound?"

"I am totally safe. But our little town is a disaster site," he added, but he demurred from describing he destruction of their new California home.

"I will call you when it's safe to return," he said. "Meanwhile enjoy the roulette tables in Nevada." He laughed and exchanged more "I love yous" and then returned to his fellow firefighters in the station. Most of them were locals. Like Jack, most had lost their homes and were distraught. Given the advance warning, almost all had advised their families to evacuate at least twelve hours before the fires invaded their neighborhoods. Part of the devastation was obviously personal. But at least an equal part was communal.

As all the firefighters privately admitted, their lovely small town was officially dead. As the force walked with gas masks in search of any living creatures, they were amazed at the ugly destruction. Everything was charred.

Nothing was standing. Even the streets were burned black. Jack had never seen anything like it and privately prayed that he would never again.

According to the latest statistics, 63 human beings officially lost their lives.

More than two hundred homes were burned to the ground. About 630 people were still missing, but the cadaver dogs were now on the case to try to match dental records. As Jack had learned from thirty years on the force, death by fire is an awful way to end one's time on earth.

With his caution, Wendy returned to California six days later. Not having actually lived through the devastation, she was awestruck by the total destruction of their home, their street, and all their neighbors' homes.

After weeks of grieving and living in a nearby hotel, Jack and Wendy decided that the only sane thing to do was to escape the devastation and move to a safer region of the United States. Florida? Hurricanes. Hawaii? Volcanoes. New York? Too crowded. Preoccupied with the downside of every community, they decided to relocate to the Midwest. Goodbye, Paradise. Hello, Normal, Illinois—far away from everything.

Within two weeks of moving into their new condo community, Jack volunteered to serve as needed on behalf of the local fire department. Over the last twelve months, there have been no emergency calls. That's Normal.

46
Merry Business

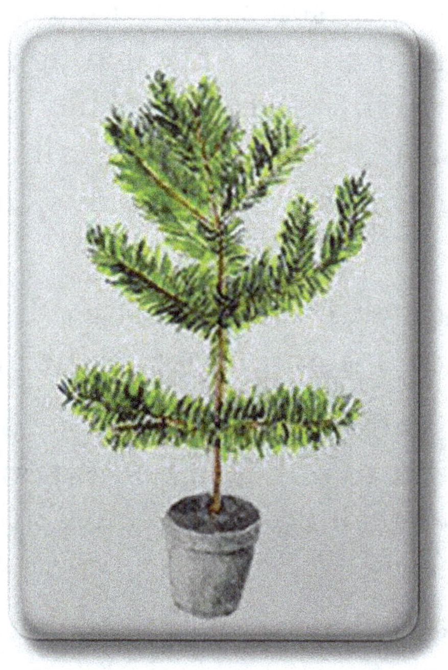

Thirty-five years ago, I inherited the Gardner Christmas Tree Farm from my dad. He had started the business forty years earlier in Berryville, Virginia, and always bragged that he was in the most joyful business on earth. As dad liked to admit, he was a happy farmer, but not a marketing mavin. Even so, we lived comfortably and had plenty of fresh air.

When I was a little kid, I loved walking through the rows of trees, smelling the balsams, and watching the workers shear the shapes into what would eventually be a perfect triangular Christmas tree for some grateful family. As a tyke, I particularly liked the scraggly baby trees, which would take about seven to eight years to reach maturity. I would normally identify a favorite or two and compare my growth to theirs every year. As I became older, I realized that a tree farm is not just a holiday business.

On our thirty-five-acre farm, we raise twenty-five thousand trees in seven varieties. It involves clearing the fields, planting seedlings, weeding, fertilizing, irrigating, moving, and shearing. Each year, four-foot-tall seedlings are planted in March.

Fortunately, it's a family business. My uncle Bob is the chief shearer. My brother-in-law Joe is in charge of irrigating and fertilizing. My wife, my aunts, and my sister work there too. They help plant the seedlings. Of course, there are some other staff members as well. Many have been here for more than a decade. In the end, everyone feels like family.

The business has changed quite a bit since I inherited from my dear dad. At that time, aluminum and other artificial trees began to invade the market.

Admittedly, I thought it might be a real threat, but eventually people missed the smell of the reality of a green Christmas. (The eco-green movement also helped).

The other big change is that many, many trees are now sold in large retailers like Target, Stew Leonard's, and Home Depot. In my dad's day, we would load some trees in a small pickup and bring them to a Boy Scout troop or a charitable operation who hoped to help people get in the Christmas spirit.

These days, many trees are loaded on large semis for delivery to the huge retailers.

However, the other big deal that is the growth of the cut-it-yourself market.

It would probably be easier to abandon this part of the business and just concentrate on the big retailers. But it wouldn't be nearly as fun, so we earmark hundreds of trees on the farm for families that wish to get in the Christmas spirit early and pick their own trees. Like our business, it is usually a family affair. Dads and moms come in SUVs with their kids and pick out the perfect tree for their living room. Some folks like the custom of cutting down their own tree. If not, my family members will gladly do it for them.

For us, it starts right after Thanksgiving and proceeds until December 23.

We also feature wreaths, garlands, and a few ornaments. But my favorite part of the farm is still the section that features little scrimpy baby trees. They are not for sale. But like I did in my early days, the little kids particularly enjoy it and identify with the ungainly physique of the specimens. Sometimes, I ask a little boy or girl their name, and I attach it on a tag to the trunk. I then invite them to come back next year, and see the progress and growth of the tree in their name. Parents seem to love this, and I'm going to guess that 80 percent of those families do return every year. What a marketing wiz I have become.

At this rate, I may need to devote more acreage each year to the families who want to visit the farm and get the Christmas tree spirit early.

47

The Secret

Shontay McGrady promised herself that it was something that she would never reveal to anyone. Just too painful. Too shameful. And then there were the legal ramifications. If ever discovered, it would mean perhaps even years of court battles and a Pandora's box of more revelations.

In her defense, Shontay had always considered it an accident. After all, she had never intended to hit the elderly woman who was obliviously and carelessly walking across the snowy road. True, the young woman had enjoyed a few glasses of wine earlier in the day at Kenyon College. But by now, she had privately convinced herself that it had no effect whatsoever on her driving ability.

It was an awful moment. At the time, she was a sophomore scholarship student in the liberal arts college once attended by Paul Newman. Typical of rural Ohio winters, the roads were slick with black ice. However, that was not enough to deter Shontay from driving back to her Queens, New York, home for Christmas break.

The old woman, later revealed to seventy-seven years old, came out of nowhere and should not have been walking aimlessly across Route 43. She should have been wearing her hearing aid and heard the blaring horn. She should have known that a moving car could not easily stop or swerve in those inclement conditions. At least that's what Shontay always told herself.

After the miserable, muffled sound of the impact, the young honors student did stop and trudge back in the blizzard toward the scene of the collision. Yes, there was blood. No, there was no apparent sign of breathing. Moreover, there was no one around. In an undeniable state of panic, Shontay pulled the woman off to a farm field and then drove twenty-three straight hours back to New York.

She was welcomed by her proud mother and father who, on a daily basis, bragged about their brilliant daughter. For years, these glowing reviews had embarrassed her, but she did understand their inherent pride and expectations.

"I hit a deer last night," she apologized to her father the following morning.

Once he was reassured that his loving daughter was uninjured (after several fictitious accounts of the accident), he took that damaged Ford Focus into his local auto body shop and made it look like new. Over the next week, Shontay heard that some villager without a family in the area had been struck by a hit-and-run driver and succumbed to a coma. Presumably, she died. Shontay had chosen not to chase this story. For a gifted, tortured student, there were already enough reminders every week.

Nightmares. They persisted for years. Through graduation from Kenyon College. Through her scholarship to Princeton Law School. Through last night.

"Ms. McGrady, can you share with us your secret to success?" It was a question the young attorney general had answered many times at college campuses. However, unlike the usual Q&A sessions, she recognized a few special guests in the auditorium. "My secret to success? My parents, who always believed in my potential."

Shontay continued. "And one more thing: everyone must overcome personal obstacles. Insecurities. Demons of one's own making. You cannot … I cannot … we cannot ever let hurdles hold us back." There was applause at this bromide. Then seven or eight more boilerplate questions about achievement. Finally, the last question surprised her.

"Professor McGrady, as a theology student, I always wonder this: do you believe that a person who carries the secret of true guilt can ever have inner peace?"

Despite Shontay's very practiced and by now even glib responses, there was an uncomfortable pause. The woman responded, "In my experience, in my heart, I believe not … and that is punishment enough."

It was as far as Shontay McGrady would ever go. As usual, she knew she would again have nightmares tonight.

48

Perfectly Placed Paddles

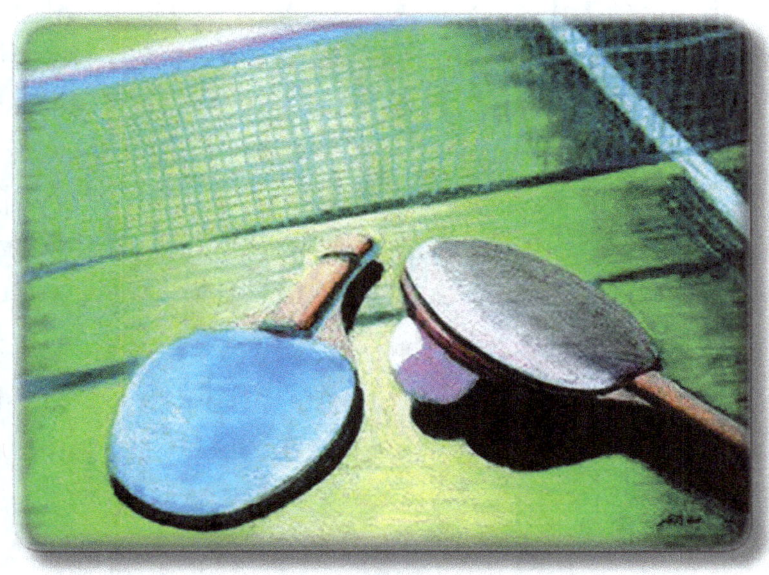

Margo Harris dusted the Ping-Pong table and sponged every inch of the surface until it was as pristinely clean as the day it was purchased. She then repositioned the paddles and the white ball in the exact spot they had been left.

Her son Ben was the last one to use the equipment.

For his thirteenth birthday, the teenager had begged his mom and dad for the table. "It's the only thing I really want."

"But you don't even play," his dad argued.

"I will."

After a hem and haw of several weeks, the parents found a top-of-the-line, indoor-outdoor, tournament-sized table at Modell's. They threw in a few paddles and balls for good measure. When the teen unwrapped his birthday packages, he literally jumped for joy; and lo and behold, Ben did play every single day for the next four months. He got to the point where he could prevail against every one of his friends, and he always easily beat his father.

151

He truly enjoyed the back-and-forth camaraderie of the game for hours and hours.

That was a year ago, before the accident. The culprit was a distracted driver who was now serving time for manslaughter. However, it happened in Margo's classic 1972 BMW 2002. She herself had sustained a broken collarbone and several fractured ribs in the driver's seat. According to the ER physicians, the seat belt had saved her life. Without ever saying as much, it was especially clear that her son's beltless ride in the other front seat exacerbated his injuries. It was immediately clear this Ben's crushed organs would make survival touch and go. After a few days on the ventilator, he passed away without ever gaining consciousness.

Of course, she blamed herself. Months of psychological therapy had barely eased the pain. She still had nightmares of the event. These used to be every-evening terrors. Lately, they occurred every other night, so in that respect, the therapy has had some effect.

Margo's routine sustained her. Every day, she recreated the last day of her son's life before that crash. It started in the bedroom, where not a single article of Ben's clothing had ever been discarded. Yes, she laundered the items, but she carefully replaced them in the exact final order. She even placed the unfolded T-shirts on the bed, just as they had been before she and Ben drove in the old BMW.

Thanks to her husband's confidential alerts to her therapist on this habit, the subject came up in Margo's sessions. However, the suggestion to repaint Ben's room resulted in Margo's month long-hiatus from therapy. So it had to proceed slowly.

Like the bedroom, the Ping-Pong table was a daily recreated shrine. When Margo put the blue paddle down for the umpteenth time, she took a few steps back to survey the tableau and remind her of better times. As she did so, she sensed the presence of her husband behind her.

"I'm here," he said quietly, and he put his arms around his once-joyful wife. The tenderness was not reciprocated, but by now he knew not to take it personally. In truth, it had nothing to do with him. He then stepped beside her and eyed the table. "It's been a year, Margo. And Ben would be so sad that this table is so idle."

The woman just continued to stare ahead.

"Maybe in his honor we should just hit ball back and forth a few times over the net." As he said this, he inched toward the paddles.

Margo immediately grasped his arm and stopped him.

"Don't touch that." And then she added a few words more firmly. "No. Not. Never." Sadly, the dad trudged back into the house to commemorate the year's anniversary of his son's death alone and in silence. As Margo lingered, she carefully lifted off the autumn leaf that had fallen on the table. After she did so, she smiled and remembered her dear son.

49

Blind Taste Test

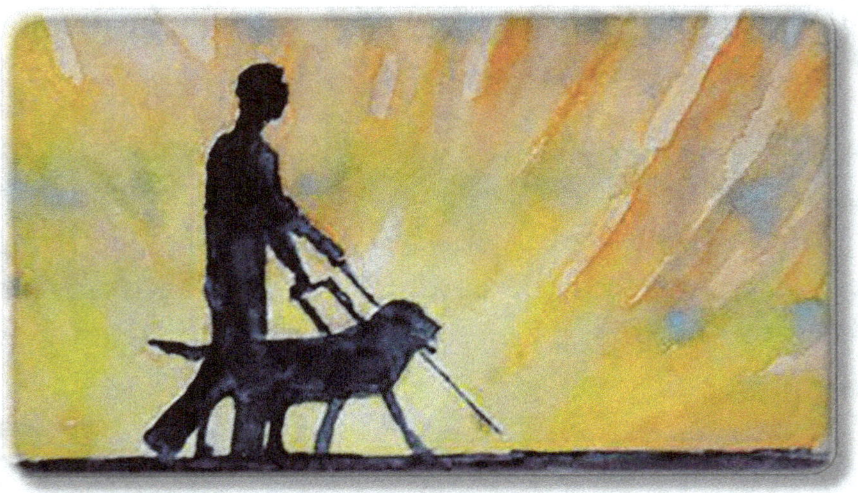

Charles Palmer had a superb command of four senses. He could hear whispers from across the street, even in a busy city metropolis. With a quick whiff, his extraordinary sense of smell could identify spices or ingredients.

He could taste a teaspoon of anything and correctly recognize the dish. His sense of touch was equally spectacular.

That extrasensory perception often happens to compensate for the loss of one key sense. In Charles's case, he lived in a dark world. As a young eighteen-year-old in Vietnam, he had been blinded by an incoming missile.

Despite many medical procedures to restore his vision, he was now 100 percent blind and had been so for the last forty-eight years. However, with his trusty guide dog, Chappy, he was able to negotiate Grand Central Station, city intersections, and side streets. Beyond the constant companionship, Chappy also helped guide the man to local bars, where he would sample a glass or two of wine a few days a week. He found it a good way to exercise his sense of smell and taste. Besides, he enjoyed this small pleasure.

On this particular day, New York City was particularly busy and provided Charles with a cacophony of entertaining sounds as he and his guard dogs walked the streets. He could hear the street entertainers sing "The more I see you, the more I want you." He overheard two businessmen obviously comparing business notes: "Take a look at these figures." Interspersed with this were far- off police sirens and jackhammers. He even heard a hard hat wolf-whistle and call out to a woman, "Hey, beautiful! Yeah, I'm looking at you."

And then he heard the sound that was music to his ears. It was the magnified slow-motion sound of a cork being pulled out of a wine bottle. He could even hear the bartender announce that the particular wine was woody and robust. A customer agreed, "Yes."

Instinctively, Charles followed the sounds and told Chappy, "I think it's this way." The guide dog knew this routine and walked the man to the cocktail lounge where Charles overheard the bartender again, "Just a slight hint of berry." When the blind man and his dog entered the place, the bartender came out to greet him and made sure he was secure in one of the bar stools.

"I heard you were serving a great Cabernet," Charles said.

"As a matter of fact, yes. Here, have a taste." The bartender put a little in a wine glass and slid it to Charles fingers.

The blind man swirled it and smelled it, and then he smiled. "Yes." The bartender then filled his glass and waited for a reaction.

Charles took another swig and then asked, "California?" This amazed the bartender. "Two thousand four?" the blind man correctly guessed. Then after another smell and taste, he confidently said, "Stag's Leap!"

"That's astonishing," the bartender gushed.

"Got a lot of practice," Charles said, and he reached into his front pocket to pull out a ten-dollar bill. Then he petted his guide dog. "Whadya say we get on the road again?" The dog whined approval, and the two of them walked out the door.

On the street, they were once again greeted with competing sounds that surrounded them. Over the roar of motorcycles, Charles could hear tourists on a nearby phone saying they had just spent the morning sightseeing. A woman was breaking up with a man, "No, I cannot see this working." Two Japanese tourists: "Wait, let me get a picture."

Against this backdrop, the blind man could also hear the magnified sound of a wine cork and a different bartender saying, "This white wine has a nice nose and a flinty taste."

"It sounds like someone is pouring a nice Cabernet Sauvignon," the blind man said to his dog. "Should we see if I am right again? Yes?" Chappy barked and led the man to the next taste test just a block from the last one.

50

Honkers

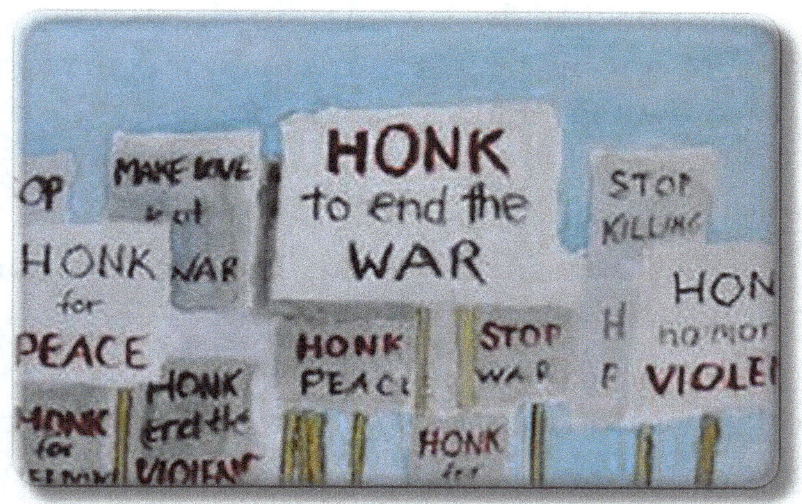

At the only major intersection of the tourist village of Amagansett, he held his hand-painted sign along with several other demonstrators. The messages variously read "Honk if you are against the war."

This ragtrag group elicited three responses. The vast majority of drivers simply passed by, either too busy to notice the placards or too distracted to participate in the argument. A smaller percentage of of cars honked in support. Approximately, an equal number of cars honked but also accompanied their alert with a middle finger out of the car window or perhaps a more guttural rebutting epithet.

Ken Rogers had been a participant in this weekly event since America's "shock and awe" incursions into Iraq. It was not an unfamiliar routine for him. As a flower child of the sixties, he had marched against Vietnam and, a decade later, against Granada. This particular protest was intended to just raise awareness and remind citizens that despite the plethora of yellow "Support Our Troops" decals on cars, not everyone in town was a hawk.

Sign in hand, he circled the loop with several other similarly minded individuals. In the midst of his loop, he met a middle-aged, grocery-toting woman who walked toward the demonstrators. "My son was a patriot," she said to Ken. "Was?" Rogers asked.

"He died in Iraq two years ago," she soberly announced.

Ken nodded when he heard the news. "I'm sorry to hear that, ma'am." Long ago, he had learned not to disparage the soldiers in combat. They were not his beef. His message was more aimed at the policymakers than the men and women in boots. At the risk of setting off a fracas, Ken added, "We believe we are patriots too, just from a different point of view."

When Ken joined the queue again, the woman continued her dialogue with him. "He believed in the cause."

"Many do. But nowadays, many don't." This was not the type of confrontation that Ken Rogers relished. From his past experiences, he understood it was difficult to swing someone to his point of view, especially someone from a military family. Such people normally believe that theirs was the only route to patriotism.

"I didn't want him to enlist," the woman added. "Even so, I think this sort of demonstration is perhaps disrespectful to his sacrifice."

Ken got out of the circle and decided to speak to the woman who seemed conflicted by emotions. "Maybe. Maybe not." He wasn't quite sure how to continue, but since she was lingering, he proceeded. "My brother died in Vietnam, and he was a brave, brave guy. But I didn't want other brothers to go through my loss. So I picked up a sign, and forty years later, I'm still carrying one. Different locale now, but the same message."

"I'm sorry for your loss," she said and walked away.

Over the next several weeks, Ken saw the same woman in her weekly grocery excursions. She would nod silently to him and go her own way.

Yesterday, she approached him again with a full bag of groceries.

"I brought you and your friends some sandwiches and soft drinks," she said, placing the bag by the curb. "I don't really think my son would object." Ken thanked her for her generosity and invited her to join in carrying a sign.

"I'm not ready for that yet," she admitted, and she handed him a ham-and-cheese sandwich.

As she did so, she quizzed Ken. "One question for you. You think any of this marching really makes a difference?"

"Sometimes I wonder," Ken Rogers answered. "And sometimes I am sure it helps, one person at a time." The woman was not quite ready to be that person. As she slowly walked away, another car honked.

The Affliction of Fine Art

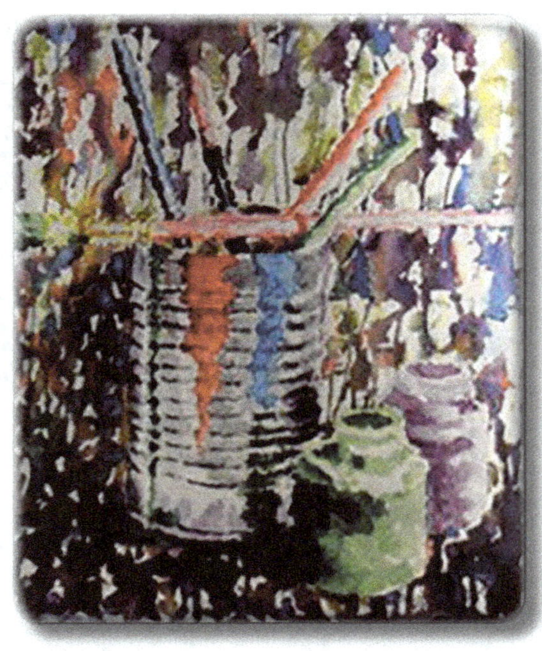

"Of all the damn diseases to contract, why this one?" Michael Barrington screamed to the heavens, but he heard no response. The diagnosis of Parkinson's disease, now confirmed by second and third opinions, was devastating news for a fine artist, especially a pro at photorealism like Barrington.

It was a renaissance career for the fifty-six-year-old baby boomers. During his marriage, he had spent several decades as a fairly successful graphic designer. When the computer revolution began to pass him by, he found therapeutic solace in his initial passion for art.

Michael knew this would be a journey—group show, juried competitions, and pay-to-display exhibitions. But it had begun to pay off. His tight, highly detailed oils attracted an audience. One of the thrills of this was that he been awarded a solo show at the Beeker Gallery, in Chelsea, New York.

And now this unrelenting, progressive tremor in his painting hand!

Discouraged, Barrington stared at empty canvasses for months, but the idea of abandoning was just too much to bear. What else could he do? In desperation, he discovered that he could mask the wobble by creating larger pieces, effectively eliminating the need for superfine detail.

"I like this evolution," Jean Marte, the curator of Beeker, told him when he brought in pieces for his second solo show. "They're loose, freer, a little less anal, if I may say so," Marte added, never one to mince words.

These larger, slightly impressionistic oils were quite a sensation. Barrington sold five large pieces and was invited again next year for another solo show.

But it was hard to retain that style as the shakes intensified over the ensuing months. What was once a straight line was now a herky-jerky, zigzag brushstroke. Dismayed, he studied the swirly impressions of van Gogh and the drips of Jackson Pollock. Without directly mimicking either one, he created a new thing: well-designed chaos.

When Barrington brought them into Beeker Gallery, Jean was jarred. "Wow. Interesting. But, Michael, you may have pushed too far."

"With fine art, there is no such thing as too far," Barrington said defensively, appearing more jittery than usual. As he spoke, he kept his shaking hands in his pants pockets, as had become his habit those days.

There were only three pictures purchased in this new genre. But it did attract the approval of several art critics and the attention of several museums—namely the Whitney and Tate Modern.

As his tremors progressively became more pronounced, Barrington had to retire the paintbrush and employ the scissors of collage, as Henri Matisse had done when palsy engulfed him. These Barrington pieces were hung in the Pompidou Center, MoMA, and dozens of other museums here and abroad.

All the while, Barrington became more reclusive. Other than his confidante and friend Jean Marte, few people know of his condition.

Michael Barrington's journey ended last year, when complications from Parkinson's claimed his life. Perhaps you read his obituary in the *New York Times*. There was no mention of his previous graphic designing career and no word of his photorealism. Just accolades of his incredible journey. By the way, at Barrington's request, there was no mention of Parkinson's disease either. As he once privately confessed to Jean Marte, "That would make what I have done the result of an affliction." At the time, Jean just smiled. "But that's exactly what it has been, Michael—the happy burden of an artist who must keep interpreting things in fresh new ways." Finally satisfied with his journey, Michael Barrington ceased shaking and closed his eyes for the last time.

52

Family Dodge

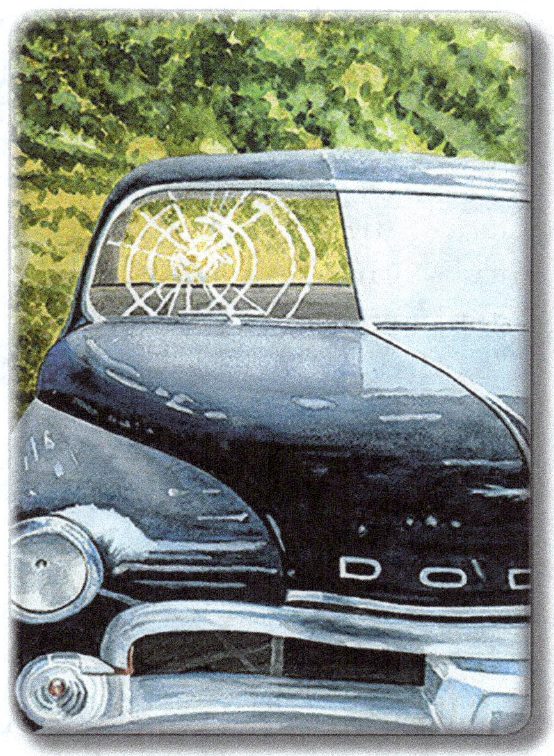

The vehicle had not been driven since Ellie's husband passed away thirty-two years ago.

Even then, the Dodge was a very old car, but it was in perfect working condition. At the time, Ellie and Albert would tool around the country roads in Shady, New York, and occasionally showcase it in nearby Woodstock.

Almost always, people would wave at the well-maintained classic and often approach the owners with admiring questions.

"What year is it?"

"She came off the assembly line in nineteen hundred and fifty-two."

"Did you buy it new?"

"Sure did."

"Cost a lot to maintain?"

"Some, but she is worth it."

All this was now a distant memory for Ellie Carmichael, who had just turned ninety. By now, there were very few neighbors who knew the old lady. She rarely ventured out of the house with a cane to tend her small backyard garden. However, most people around the rural village knew that small cottage on Wittenberg Road, with the old Dodge parked under the big maple.

For the first few decades, she regularly gave the car a good cleaning. But after that brutal snowstorm that resulted in the cracked windshield and Ellie's first hip replacement, those rejuvenations became less frequent. The burden of that maintenance now fell on her only son, Richard, who would visit almost every season from Albany.

"Mom, why don't we unload this rattletrap?" he sometimes asked, apparently oblivious to his mother's emotional attachment to the thing. "At this point, it's just a financial drain, especially since you don't even drive the damn thing."

Ellie never chose to answer this request verbally. Her wistful looks and frustrated sighs were always enough to spur Richard to grab the bucket and sponge and make the car look relatively fresh, at least for several weeks. At the conclusion of this ritual, the son would normally guide his mother out of the house to view the antique. They would then share a bit, and she would reminisce about the good old days. This routine continued for eight years, until this spring.

"I'm thinking it's time to say goodbye to the Dodge," she announced to her son.

Reversing roles, Richard did not respond verbally. "It's old. It's broken. Maybe it's time to just let it go."

Richard grabbed the bucket and sponge and shook his head. "When I give it a good wash, it will feel like new."

That afternoon, the two of them paged through old photo albums and discussed the early years of her marriage with Albert. It was a good marriage made even better by the birth of a son after years of trying. She told Richard how proud she was that he had built a life in Albany, although she wished he was geographically a little closer. The topic of the old Dodge was not again addressed. Later that night, they had dinner in her bedroom, since Ellie was feeling too weak to move to the dining room table.

It was their last meal together.

In the middle of the night, she peacefully passed in the presence of her dear son and her beloved Dodge.

Three months later, the little homestead of Wittenberg Road was on the market. Given its bucolic setting and proximity to Woodstock, it was an attractive property for many weekenders from New York City. One interested couple from Manhattan came to view the cottage for the second time this weekend.

"Does the old Dodge come with the place?" the prospective buyer eagerly asked.

"Afraid not," Richard wistfully replied. "She's family. And she's coming with me to her new home in Albany."

53

Jukebox Heaven

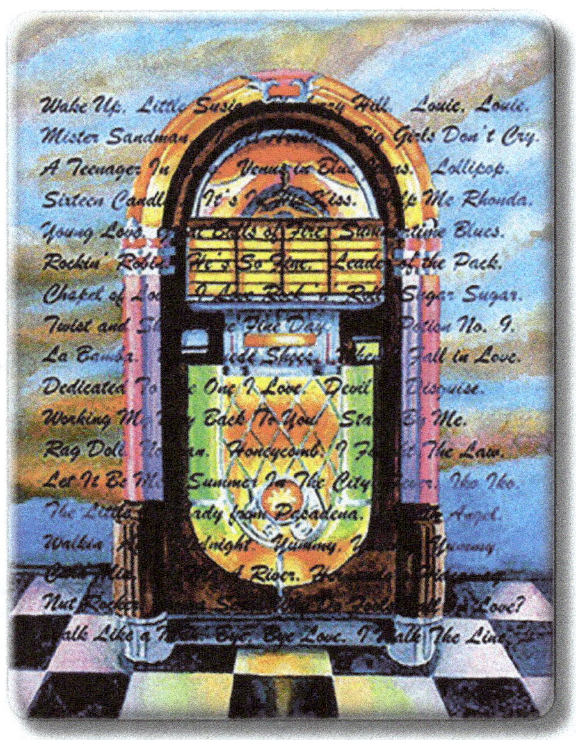

Unlike the typical knock, knock, there was a rhythmic, syncopated knock on the door, with a few bangs at the top, countered by a bass beat on the bottom. Within five seconds, a bearded man in a white robe opened that thick wooden portal and then the pearlescent iron gate. He extended his hand to the newcomer and introduced himself. "I am Peter," the greeter succinctly said, as if his first name should be sufficient. "And you are …" the questioner put on his reading glasses, took his clipboard, and scanned down the computer printout.

"I'm Johnny," the visitor soberly answered, thinking that first names were undoubtedly the custom in this new venue.

Peter looked at the man dressed in black. "Uh-huh," he responded skeptically, and he continued to turn the pages of his check-in files.

"What has been your business? Your impact? In other words, what qualifies you?"

"I don't know," Johnny humbly answered. "I just made music the best I could."

Peter flipped a few more pages on his clipboard and then seemed to recognize the visitor. The reservationist could not resist a slight wry smile.

He then looked back at the modest man, just to make sure the dossier and the image matched. "Well, you have definitely had a few stumbles along the way."

"More than a few," Johnny answered.

"But you made amazing music," Peter quickly responded, and then he looked at his checklist. "We appreciate that here. What was the purpose? Fame?"

Johnny chortled. "Nah, it's always a long, hard slog to fame."

"Money?"

"There was no money until I was in my fifties."

"Girls?"

"There was only one girl who mattered. Her name was June."

By now Peter was busily marking the computer sheet with his own grading scheme. As Johnny stood before him, the receptionist mumbled, "Some troubles. Made amends. Jukebox hits. Yes, jukebox. One. Two. Three. Four. Free concerts. That counts. That's big." Peter then high-fived the visitor and waved him forward.

"What's jukebox have to do with it?" Johnny innocently asked.

"It means you brought pleasure and above-the-earth melodies to millions."

"And that counts?"

"Big time. It's godlike, and those concerts at Folsom were major. As the Big Guy says, 'Whatever you do for the least of my brethren, you do for me.'" Peter then gave a thumbs-up gesture and encouraged him to speed through the portal.

Never one to bask in the spotlight, Johnny squinted in the glare as he walked through the gates with the man called Peter and felt a new creative inspiration.

"Is June here?" he asked.

"Yes, of course. She put up with you."

"What about Richie Valens?"

"Definitely."

"Elvis?"

"He was an amazing talent and good to his staff. So on balance, yes."

"What about John Lennon?"

"Well, the Big Guy didn't particularly like the fact that he said his group was bigger than Jesus, but he did understand the ironic critique and loved 'Hey Jude.'"

After a pause, Johnny viewed the sunrise and great jukebox in the sky. He then asked the receptionist, "So I'm in?"

"Two conditions," Peter said. "You've got to lose that 'man in black' thing."

John put on the white robe that the angels on his right and left extended to him. "And you've got to promise to be good in your own way. No transgressions. No failures. No excuses," Peter demanded.

Johnny took the guitar the angel extended to him and began singing the iconic song "I Walk the Line." The vast mile-long audience—many reformed members of Folsom Prison—cheered and were again so happy to be in his company.